Intellectual Disability in a Post-Neoliberal World

Jennifer Clegg • Richard Lansdall-Welfare

Intellectual Disability in a Post-Neoliberal World

palgrave
macmillan

Jennifer Clegg
Living with Disability Research Centre
La Trobe University
Melbourne, VIC, Australia

Richard Lansdall-Welfare
Nottingham, Nottinghamshire, UK

ISBN 978-3-031-57944-8   ISBN 978-3-031-57945-5   (eBook)
https://doi.org/10.1007/978-3-031-57945-5

This Palgrave Macmillan imprint is published by the registered company Springer Nature Switzerland AG.
The registered company address is: Gewerbestrasse 11, 6330 Cham, Switzerland

Paper in this product is recyclable.

Acknowledgements

A legion of warm-hearted, open-minded people has shaped this endeavour. We thank all those with intellectual disability and their relatives who have shared lives, hopes, and efforts with us; the direct care staff who were willing to try doing something new that had been developed in another country—often the Netherlands—or with other mental health groups; and the national research funders and Nottingham's health service managers who supported innovation in unimaginative times. We also thank individuals who encouraged our early steps, especially John Ballatt, who gave a close reading of a very early draft and stayed in conversation about the changes as they unfolded. Other thoughtful and incisive encouragers across the world at different times include Christine Bigby, Angus Buchanan, Bill Fulford, John Hall, Jacques Heijkoop, Tony Holland, Andrew Jahoda, Jo Jones, Patrick McKearney, Herman Meininger, Gareth Morgan, Elizabeth Murphy, Hans Reinders, Carlo Schuengel, Paula Sterkenburg, and Graham Turpin. Long may they all continue to expand the ways it is possible to think.

Ethics Approval All references to anonymised human participants originally published in research papers by Clegg with other authors derives from research that was approved by a National Health Service Research Ethics Committee in the East Midlands, UK.

Contents

1

Why Ideas Matter

Abstract This chapter lays out the conceptual basis of the book. It introduces a fundamental position: that recurring problems flag up what needs to be reflected upon and changed, and provide essential foci for a new conceptualisation. It outlines two tools for thinking about them deployed throughout the book: examples from real life, and the philosophy of creativity developed by Deleuze. It ends with an overarching account that identifies options for renewal and invites all people who think change is overdue to join in its creation.

Keywords Intellectual disability • Practice concepts • Creativity • Deleuze

1 Introduction

Instead of the usual order let us start at the very end. The conclusion to Chap. 6 is called *Everything seems impossible until it's done*, a saying that has been attributed to politicians from Pliny the Elder to Nelson Mandela.

This upbeat statement suggests that, however entrenched things seem to be, change will come once people dare to imagine what a better situation would look like.

Our attempts to envisage that change started in 2010 when Nottingham's Counterpoint conference brought a small group of international researchers and clinicians together to reflect on where we were and how change might happen. Three fine days summarising and discussing pre-circulated presentations identified the following themes (Clegg, 2010). The need to change language so that it better reflects and respects the diversity of people with intellectual disability and their modes of existence, and seeing with a clearer eye to enable new approaches to emerge and flourish. There was attention to history as well as the immediate contexts people live in. Since examining the past reveals how things could be other than they are, histories of the discipline are also drawn on to see how moments of radical revision were precipitated by accumulating contradictions about intellectual disability that finally became too big to ignore. Observing that two such moments occurred during the twentieth century, Gleeson (2010) predicted that a third such moment of change was due.

We also watched a film that illustrated an experiment led by influential British psychologist Jack Tizard (1969) in his Brooklands project, which offered family-like care and compared it to institutional care. Counterpoint speakers were struck by what was visible but not measured: the risk-taking available to children playing in a garden, who walked across logs and other things they could fall from; the warmth and animation between them and staff. Speakers also interrogated normalisation: since value is not fixed, why is belonging to an in-group better than belonging to an out-group? We left hoping that positive change was imminent (but did not in fact happen), and believing that this was less likely to emerge from system reconstruction than from local projects involving new roles and ways that people with intellectual disabilities can thrive.

The clinical experiences, ideas, and research evidence about people with intellectual disability that this book assembles add to the argument made in Counterpoint for a radical re-conceptualisation. Yet saying it should and could be different invites incredulity. Do you not know that it is impossible to question sacred beliefs like choice? Surely you are not challenging the widespread view that positive behavioural support is the answer to everybody who is distressed or dysregulated, or would be if only staff did it properly? Moreover, since scandals break out with depressing regularity in staffed services across the developed world, why wouldn't closing them all and moving everybody into the community be the right response?

The following chapters track the way that neoliberal principles have negatively influenced services for people with intellectual disabilities and the parents and staff who support them. They also describe viable and possible alternatives. Yet challenging existing goals challenges aspirations that have become sources of hope for parents, professionals, and intellectual disability advocacy groups. What if people with intellectual disability could:

- Get jobs that lift them out of isolation and poverty?
- Have their needs met by speaking truth to power?
- Find acceptance in mainstream settings?

Such aspirations radiate a positive energy that keeps people in difficult circumstances going. Understandable reluctance to abandon hope fuels the argument made by many that these sunny uplands are achievable if only everybody tries hard enough. Yet, far from advancing these goals, change is in the opposite direction. Good personalised residential services for people with intellectual disabilities are being dismantled, even in well-funded Nordic countries (Tøssebro et al., 2012; Bjorne, 2020). While people sometimes do still live in physically better homes, once their parents die many find themselves utterly alone (Power & Bartlett, 2019).

We proceed cautiously, because the most important knowledge of how to understand, care for, and be with people who have intellectual disabilities is held by those involved with the widely differing kinds of people in this group—and, in the main, only by them. That knowledge is rarely articulated in an environment fixed on the experiences of individuals, rather than the negotiations that unfold between them and those who provide support and care. Only the very brave lift the lid off relationships of care, because they are complicated. At best, moments of insight and delight enlarge our knowledge of the many ways of being human.

However, boredom, distaste, frustration, or fear are rarely far away. Artist Paula Rego portrayed the way carer and cared-for are similar and sometimes trapped by each other. In her *Jane Eyre* suite of paintings, Rego explored the similarity between the 'mad woman' locked in Mr Rochester's attic and her carer: both dishevelled, uncomfortable, poorly dressed, resigned. In other paintings Rego depicted her own less-than-admirable feelings as she dressed her husband Victor, who died of multiple sclerosis after a very long illness. Maria Balshaw, director of the Tate art gallery, described Rego as an uncompromising artist of extraordinary imaginative power, who uniquely revolutionised the way in which women's lives and stories are represented.

The following observation from a creative and energising pioneer in the field provided a significant starting-point.

2   Little Hedgehogs of Doubt

Psychiatrists are for the most part bent… on doing their best for patients according to current methods and theories, without stopping to pick up and examine the little hedgehogs of doubt that sit by the therapist's path. Aubrey Lewis (1967, p. 199)

Lewis (1900–1975) was one of the earliest British psychiatrists to take an interest in intellectual disability, and to broaden medicine by welcoming psychological research. He highlighted the importance of questioning—yet its difficulty. Lewis encouraged clinical investigators to be fully alive to the rigorous demands of research, and equally alive to the extreme complexity of the problems they face. Both have been central to the authors' career-long search for better ways to respond to distressed adults with intellectual disability, and to the parents and staff involved with those individuals. The social and medical scientists Lewis encouraged to pick up 'hedgehogs of doubt' were clinician researchers like Ann & Alan Clarke, Michael Rutter, and Jack Tizard, who posed and answered unique questions. Making no assumption that colleagues would agree with them they gained the ear of government, changed practice in the UK, founded the international congress IASSIDD and became influential figures within the WHO, UN and OECD.

We started looking for hedgehogs lurking in the undergrowth that need to be picked up and examined. Deciding to examine the scandals that regularly unfold in developed as well as low and middle-income countries, one of us (Clegg & Jones, 2017) convened a symposium with colleagues at a European congress. This turned out to be so popular, members of the audience struggled to find any space on the floor to sit. The germ of this book was sown.

3 Two Tools for Thinking

Real-Life Examples

Creating anything new requires deep thought—but about what? Billig (2019) argued that social science writing is at its clearest and best when grounded in real-life examples. Since we have been both researchers and clinicians, many of the issues described arose from reflecting on the hundreds of people with intellectual disabilities we have met during 30-year careers, while of course respecting confidentiality. The following insight from psychoanalytic psychotherapist Valerie Sinason sets the tone. She asked why intellectual disability service staff act as though, if they work hard enough, all people with intellectual disability can become independent. She went on to observe that the people themselves not only resist this idea, some handicap themselves further by developing secondary disabilities:

> Opening your eyes to admitting you look, sound, walk, talk, move or think differently takes great reserves of courage, honesty and toleration of envy. It can be easier to behave like the village idiot and make everyone laugh than to expose the unbearable discrepancy between normal and not normal. (Sinason, 1986, p. 132)

This mismatch between self and self-presentation brings new levels of complexity. The people with intellectual disabilities that we have in mind are the 40% who come to the attention of services because there is a difficulty or issue that troubles them and those who support them.

To help readers imagine the situations we are describing, ideas and themes are illustrated throughout by brief reference to real people. These mainly refer to individuals who consented to research publication and whose anonymised information is already in the public domain. Only sketching in issues relevant to the research is sometimes criticised as reductive, because people are always more than the sum of their problems. This is of course true, but a rounded account that describes a person in a specific situation with unique interests presents far too high a risk of identifiability. We choose to safeguard anonymity by limiting descriptions to the least detail necessary to understand the matter at hand. Wherever possible, we also include more rounded accounts published by family members to flesh out the narrative.

Hurdles to understanding how physical and mental health issues combine and impact people with intellectual disabilities were detailed in an award-winning paper by Wark and Kingstone (2019). They demonstrated this complex group's unique needs by analysing a four-decade case-history of a non-verbal man with severe intellectual disability. His case had not been selected because of complexity, but simply because he had lived in one place that kept good records. The authors accepted that psychiatric diagnoses can change over time, but not to the degree observed. Non-specialist doctors had changed this man's diagnosis from a genetic condition, Prader-Willi syndrome, to 'chronic' autism, not autism, anxiety, depression, and schizophrenia. Such diagnoses are required to release funding but can result in inappropriate medication and management. The man also had lifelong constipation, chronic bronchitis and pneumonia, late-onset epilepsy and kidney disease. The authors argued that pain management was clearly required throughout his life, but medication to address this had only been prescribed late in his life. Repeated rejections of the medical model as inappropriate for this group may cause us not to identify the range of physical conditions that often require treatment, the difficulty of diagnosing people who are unable to describe how their body feels, and the complex ways that medicines may be administered:

The medication regimens of people with IDD are almost twice as complex as the regimens of people prescribed medications but who do not have IDD. Importantly, the differences in regimens are not only due to a higher number of medications... but also in the frequency of dose administrations ... by routes other than by mouth ... (&) special instructions for administration. (Erickson et al., 2018, p. 355)

So, people with intellectual disability have different and complicated health as well as social needs. Everything needs to be attended to in the search for possibilities that express new kinds of hope for all people with intellectual disability, and for the families and staff involved with them.

A significant matter that requires attention as we work towards ideas that fit real-life people is the fact that this population changes. In his end-of-career interview recorded for the British Psychological Society's oral history archive (Clarke & Clarke, 2007), Alan Clarke emphasised that people described as mentally handicapped in 2007 were already quite different from those he and Ann had helped to get jobs in the 1950s. The population had become more disabled.

This trend towards the population becoming more severely intellectually disabled continues to the present day. The introduction of safe prenatal testing has led to far fewer people with Down's syndrome being born in countries where testing is available and terminations legal: more than 80% of foetuses diagnosed with Down's syndrome through prenatal testing resulted in terminations (Wilson, 2017). This is a major change because people with Down's syndrome used to be the biggest single group within intellectual disability, about 20% of the population. Their impairment is usually mild-moderate and their behaviour rarely challenging. Internationally, most depictions of someone with an intellectual disability finding paid work, getting married, and making their voice heard through performance or politics feature somebody who has Down's syndrome. At the opposite end of the spectrum, developments in neonatology and medicine (Emerson, 2009) have clearly resulted in accelerating growth in the number of people with profound and multiple disabilities surviving infancy and reaching adulthood in England.

The relative absence of multiply disabled people in the civic space, and regular representation of intellectual disability by people who have

Down's syndrome, probably contribute to the majority of the population underestimating the impact of limited abstract thinking and difficulties in communication and self-determination (Clegg & Bigby, 2017). As a result of substantial brain impairments combining with physical and mental health problems, many members of this group require sustained and sometimes protective care. Many parents have no help and are chronically sleep-deprived, and the older ones are in significantly poorer health themselves (literature reviewed in Chap. 5). Of course, we should remain concerned about the quality of life of each individual, which is the focus of current services; but we should ensure that the difficulties experienced by staff and parents who provide such care are understood and addressed as well.

A Philosophy of Creativity: Deleuze

Lewis' comment about 'hedgehogs' that lurk beside the clinician's path connects with this twentieth-century French philosopher's argument that important issues flag their significance by repeating, and that creating the new should not leap away from what is. Rather, creativity should emerge from the important matters at hand by taking a deep and different look at them. Deleuze's lifetime interest in creativity was expressed in what he called his first real book of philosophy, *Difference and Repetition* (Deleuze, 1968), and also in his final book, *What is Philosophy?* (Deleuze & Guattari, 1991).

Unfortunately, mention of Deleuze in mental health contexts tends to elicit an assumption that this refers (or *should* refer) to two other books he co-authored with Guattari, a French psychiatrist who worked at a radical therapeutic community outside Paris. *Anti-Oedipus* and *A Thousand Plateaus* address psycho-analysis and schizophrenia: difficult reads, their content has little relevance to our project.

While *What is Philosophy?* also attributed co-authorship to Guattari, according to their biographer Dosse (2010) Guattari played no part in its composition. "Both a very personal project and something of a crowning moment in the philosopher's life, *What is Philosophy?* was manifestly written by Deleuze alone, but he agreed to a co-author credit with Guattari as a tribute to their intense friendship" (Dosse, 2010, p. 456).

Recognising the need to expand our conceptual vocabulary to avoid being constrained by the sense that things already make, Deleuze elaborated a new kind of thought: one that eschews judgement and prefers learning. The two works by Deleuze on which the present book rests address the creation of new concepts. When we notice repetitions, then look at them long enough to become able to also see how they differ, we start to change the conceptual lenses that shape what we see. A Deleuzean philosopher observed: "Thinking is a nomadic activity which takes place in the transitions between potentially contradictory positions" (Braidotti, 2006, p. 29).

The conceptual nets that Deleuze threw over a chaotic world feature duration and interaction. He theorised what 'bodies in motion' (people in relationship, and their interactions with all living things and ideas in their habitat) generate over time. A brilliant study of how to address the sexual needs of disabled people unfolds the difference between taking an individual and a 'bodies in motion over time' position (Kulick & Rydström, 2015). Describing in unflinching detail the unprivate universe in which people with disabilities live, one person said he did not simply 'go to the toilet': elimination involved 'other people's hands being in his private hairs' every day.

So, creating new understandings of intellectual disability is an important focus: where it comes from, how it is fostered. Yet creativity is difficult, a struggle. The following extract captures Deleuze's lifetime engagement with it:

> Fromanger [a painter] and Deleuze became fast friends .... Deleuze asked the artist how he painted, how he worked, and his creative process .... How he managed to put things on a canvas that was initially white. I told him, "You see it as blank, but in fact it's black .... It's black with everything every painter has painted before me ...." Deleuze went back to this idea virtually word for word in *What is Philosophy*: "The painter does not paint on an empty canvas, and neither does the writer write on a blank page; but the page or canvas is already so covered with pre-existing, pre-established cliches that first you have to erase, clean, flatten, even shred, so as to let in a breath of air." (Dosse, 2010, pp. 441–2)

The suffocating power of pre-existing cliches resonates with Aubrey Lewis' criticism of too much certainty because certainty prevents vital questioning. Certainty in intellectual disability was also challenged by US iconoclast Burton Blatt (Taylor & Blatt, 1999) because it inhibits the natural evolution of thought. When accumulated contradictions do provoke a revolution that addresses shortcomings in the existing position in intellectual disability, the danger is that whatever replaced the previous 'magic answer' soon turns into a new, unchallengeable truth.

The difficulty of clearing a space to think about intellectual disability anew *and* keeping it open was articulated by another philosopher, Carlson (2010), who observed that apparent conceptual shifts in intellectual disability are rarely true changes. Rather, it has been an oscillating body of knowledge trapped inside four binary positions:

- Quantitative–Qualitative
- Static–Dynamic
- Protective–Productive
- Visible–Invisible

Since dichotomies encourage simplification and misconception that inhibit debate, twenty-first-century ethicists have urged their abandonment. Discussion needs to become "less about polar right and wrong actions, but instead choosing the better action from a range of possibilities" (Sadler et al., 2015, p. 7). Yet we will show that for staff, adherence to long-standing values like autonomy and choice is a moral imperative: people act as if expressing allegiance to them is required for peers to consider them good people. We invite those in a position to open a window and welcome a new breath of air to explore the Deleuzean approach to creativity.

4   The Book in a Nutshell

Why we need to change from an individualist to a relational perspective, and what that could be like, was steadily revealed as we stopped to pick up three prickly 'hedgehogs' that can be found lying alongside the paths of intellectual disability:

- How care becomes scandalously corrupted and what to do about it?
- Resolving a paradox: why services meet emotional distress with a behavioural response?
- How parents and services for adults could work better together?

The chapters examine each of these by bringing conceptual analysis, experiential knowledge, and practice-relevant research into dialogue. Each is polyphonic, deploying or developing ideas from the growing number of disciplines that sit in the margins: anthropology (McKearney, 2020), epidemiology (Wilkinson & Pickett, 2018), geography (Gleeson, 2010), history (Toms, 2013), philosophy (Reinders, 2000), physical health (Mol, 2008), and politics (Fine & Saad-Filho, 2017).

Chapter 2 prepares the ground for change by examining neoliberal individualism's ideology, so that the difficult process of rethinking can start. Hanging above us as invisibly as the air we breathe, most practitioners find it difficult to see neoliberal concepts as assertions of belief or principles because they circulate as self-evident, taken-for-granted-goods. Noticing and seeing beyond them is effortful, but allowing the market to determine political decisions has no truck with the weak and vulnerable, who cannot compete on equal terms.

Our exploration reviews what neoliberalism is, how it is maintained, and why it is so difficult to erect alternatives able to stand up to it. The development then virtual demise of family therapy in intellectual disability is a case in point. It developed mainly in the UK as a number of professionals working in intellectual disability also qualified as systemic and family psychotherapists. This led to the publication of a book edited by Baum and Lyngaard (2006) and articles in relevant journals. However, despite considerable interest in this approach from post-graduate students training in clinical psychology, output has dwindled as the first generation of qualified family therapists has retired. The last article about intellectual disability published in the *Journal of Family Therapy* was in 2012; the last in Family Process was in 2017. In environments steeped in neoliberal values, other perspectives with promise have tended to dribble through the fingers like sand. This book seeks to change that.

Our first hedgehog is addressed in Chap. 3: the *scandals* that are a recurring feature of services for people with intellectual disabilities, and the one thing that members of the public know about this group. Media outrage and a scramble for stories is followed by inquiries and the passage of laws intended to reduce restrictive practices. These appear to be powerful but have been weak at engendering change. We challenge the belief that malpractice occurs because institutional staff are inherently abusive, with its implicit corollary that closing every institution will make it disappear.

The hedgehog picked up in Chap. 4 is a paradox. Why, throughout the last 50 years, have distressed people with intellectual disability who struggle to manage their chaotic emotions been met with behavioural, rather than emotional, interventions? It stands in contrast to policy responses to children or adults with mental health problems. Happily, research on the positive impact of emotion-focussed assessments and interventions in intellectual disability is growing exponentially.

Chapter 5 addresses a rarely explored topic: tensions in the relationship between parents and professionals. While there is research on the relationship between services and parents of children with intellectual disabilities, very little consideration is given to the interaction between services and parents of adults. This chapter develops a position from politics research. Rather than continuing to advocate for individual empowerment, and its limited scope for improving the situation of people with intellectual disabilities and that of their parents, the truly radical approach disrupts the status quo. It attends to similarities between people with intellectual disability, parents, and direct care staff, and seeks to create communities of solidarity that connect them all.

The final Chap. 6 unfolds an imagined post-neoliberal world that can accommodate heterogeneity, and complexity. We suggest polyphony as one way to describe this new era, where each group and discipline follows its own line, but their tunes start to resemble one another until a satisfying coalescence is reached. This coalescence allows for not one but many kinds of relationship. It brackets some things (our indignation about cruelty) to focus on supporting staff to retain their humanity despite spending their working day with people who range from relatively unresponsive to frightening. It argues for reducing administrative attention to uncreative activities (monitoring agencies; preparation for jobs that are not there) to make room and resource for the new (much better support, high-quality clinical supervision and training for direct care staff working with dysregulated people; new, sustainable community groups). We are not working towards fulfilling a blueprint, but evolving shared possibilities.

5   How to Read It

The book is intended to be read as a whole, but each chapter is self-contained and concludes with its own set of references to make each of them useful to university courses that cover only some of these topics. It is aimed primarily at practice researchers, research-minded clinicians and students training in those fields, and final-year undergraduates thinking of doing so; families seeking alternative perspectives will also find ideas to inspire. Those of a practical bent may prefer to skip Chap. 2's explanation of neoliberalism until they feel the need to understand their context better. Those readers might cut to the chase and start with how to think differently about the scandals that happen repeatedly, how to address emotional rather than behavioural lives, and how to improve the relationship between families and services.

References

Baum, S., & Lyngaard, H. (Eds.). (2006). *Intellectual disabilities: A systemic approach*. Karnac.

Billig, M. (2019). *More examples, less theory*. Cambridge University Press.

Bjorne, P. (2020). As if living like others: An idealisation of life in group homes for people with intellectual disability. *Journal of Intellectual & Developmental Disability, 45*(4), 337–343. https://doi.org/10.3109/1366825 0.2020.1793451

Braidotti, R. (2006). *Transpositions*. Polity.

Carlson, L. (2010). *The Faces of Intellectual Disability: Philosophical Reflections*. Indiana University Press.

Clarke, A. M., & Clarke, A. D. B. (2007, August 29). Interview by M. Wang [Audio recording]. BPS History of Psychology Centre Oral History Project (AUD/002/OHP 25). J.C. Kenna Audio Archive, BPS, London.

Clegg, J., & Bigby, C. (2017). Debates about dedifferentiation: Twenty-First century thinking about people with intellectual disabilities as distinct members of the disability group. *Research and Practice in Intellectual and Developmental Disabilities, 4*(1), 80–97.

Clegg, J. A. (2010). Emerging themes. *Journal of Intellectual Disability Research, 54*(Suppl. 1), 73–78.

Clegg, J. A., & Jones, J. (2017). Scandals: Where and why they happen. Symposium 'Equipping staff to meet challenging behaviour', *11th congress of European Congress on Mental Health in Intellectual Disability*, Luxembourg.

Deleuze, G. (1968). *Difference and repetition* (P. Patton 2004, English Trans.). Continuum.

Deleuze, G., & Guattari, F. (1991). *What is Philosophy?* (G. Burchell & H. Tomlinson 1994, English Trans.). Verso.

Dosse, F. (2010). *Gilles Deleuze & Felix Guattari: Intersecting lives* (D. Glassman, Trans.) Columbia University Press.

Emerson, E. (2009). Relative child poverty, income inequality, wealth, and health. *Tizard Learning Disability Review, 14*, 49–55.

Erickson, S., Nicaj, D., & Barron, S. (2018). Complexity of medication regimens of people with intellectual and developmental disabilities. *Journal of Intellectual & Developmental Disability, 43*(3), 351–361. https://doi.org/1 0.3109/13668250.2017.1350836

Fine, B., & Saad-Filho, A. (2017). 13 things you need to know about neoliberalism. *Critical Sociology, 43*(4–5), 685–706. https://doi.org/10.1177/ 0896920516655387

Gleeson, B. (2010). Counterpoints of care: Two moments of struggle. *Journal of Intellectual Disability Research, 54*(Suppl. 1), 5–15.

Kulick, D., & Rydström, J. (2015). *Loneliness and its opposite*. Duke University Press.

Lewis, A. (1967). *The state of psychiatry: Essays and addresses*. Science House.

McKearney, P. (2020). What escapes persuasion: Why intellectual disability troubles 'dependence' in liberal societies. *Medical Anthropology*. https://doi. org/10.1080/01459740.2020.1805741

Mol, A. (2008). *The logic of care: Health and the problem of patient choice*. Routledge.

Power, A., & Bartlett, R. (2019). Ageing with a learning disability: Care and support in the context of austerity. *Social Science & Medicine, 231*, 55–61. https://doi.org/10.1016/j.socscimed.2018.03.028

Reinders, H. S. (2000). *The future of the disabled in liberal society: An ethical analysis*. University of Notre Dame Press.

Sadler, J., van Staden, C. W., & Fulford, K. W. M. (2015). Introduction: Why an Oxford handbook of psychiatric ethics? In J. Z. Sadler, K. Fulford, & C. W. van Staden (Eds.), *The Oxford handbook of psychiatric ethics* (Vol. 1, pp. 3–29). Oxford University Press.

Sinason, V. (1986). Secondary mental handicap and its relationship to trauma. *Psychoanalytic Psychotherapy, 2*(2), 131–154. https://doi.org/10.1080/02668738600700141

Taylor, S. J. & Blatt, S. D. (1999). *In Search of the Promised Land: The Collected Papers of Burton Blatt*. American Association on Mental Retardation.

Tizard, J. (1969). *Mentally handicapped children growing up*. https://vimeo.com/ondemand/brooklandsexperiment

Toms, J. (2013). *Mental hygiene and psychiatry in modern Britain*. Palgrave Macmillan.

Tøssebro, J., Bonfils, I. S., Teittinen, A., Tideman, M., Traustadóttir, R., & Vesala, H. T. (2012). Normalization fifty years beyond—Current trends in the Nordic countries. *Journal of Policy and Practice in Intellectual Disabilities, 9*(2), 134–146.

Wark, S., & Kingstone, M. (2019). The complexity of lifelong comorbidities with severe intellectual disability. *Journal of Intellectual & Developmental Disability, 454*(4), 431–438. https://doi.org/10.3109/1366825 0.2018.1481735

Wilkinson, R., & Pickett, K. (2018). *The inner level: How more equal societies reduce stress, restore sanity and improve everyone's well-being*. Allen Lane.

Wilson, R. (2017). Contemporary forms of eugenics. *Bioethics and Philosophy*. https://doi.org/10.1002/9780470015902.a0027075

2

Noticing Neoliberalism

Abstract This chapter specifies the fundamental concepts of neoliberalism, and tracks their baleful effects on people with intellectual disabilities. These include over-estimation of their abilities which relieves social care agencies from any responsibility for imagining what an acceptable or meaningful adult life without work could be. Instead, individuals with intellectual disability are left to imagine and 'choose' it for themselves. People often struggle to recognise neoliberal ideas and the anomalies they generate, which occasionally leads them to misunderstand research findings, in itself a demonstration of the power of neoliberal ideology.

Keywords Intellectual disability • Neoliberalism • Choice • Over-estimation

Neoliberal ideology's focus on the individual and their exercise of autonomy is particularly problematic for people with intellectual disability who, as psychologist and attachment specialist Schuengel (research described in Chap. 4) and philosopher Reinders (2000) both emphasise, are fundamentally people who need people. A substantial proportion are not safe to be left alone. Yet, despite the baleful implications of its 'devil take the hindmost' approach to all who require support to live a good life, neoliberalism's brief but illusory economic success has made politicians on the left as well as the right pursue it. These are its characteristics.

1   Neoliberal Ideology

Neoliberal democracy undermined the foundations of democracy itself: structures of representation became unresponsive, public policy became both rigid and indifferent to the majority, and the state signalled that class-based collectivities would no longer be recognised…. In the end, it was each person for themselves. (Saad-Filho, 2021, p. 134)

Sociologists and historians have identified the following core characteristics, drawing primarily on researchers Fine and Saad-Filho (2017) and Stedman Jones (2012). Further details are in Clegg and Lansdall-Welfare (2020):

1. The originator of neoliberal economics, Hayek (1960), was an Austrian economist who taught in London (1930–1950) and then Chicago (1950–1962) before returning to Austria. Overshadowed by Keynesian economics for much of his career, being awarded the Nobel Prize for Economics in 1974 resurrected his reputation. Political and economic turmoil of the late 1970s created a policy vacuum in Britain and the United States into which first UK Prime Minister Margaret Thatcher (1979–1990) and then US President Ronald Reagan (1980–1989) inserted Hayek's ideas. His key argument was that state intervention leads to loss of liberty. He considered markets to be wiser than individuals, and government interference to make things worse not better.
2. Neoliberalism has had three distinct phases: 1920 to 1950, 1950 to 1980, and 1980 to date, with the current third phase moving neoliberalism beyond economics into politics and culture. Simple, powerful ideas established it in both the US and the UK. 'Workfare' in the US emphasised self-sufficiency and coerced welfare recipients to seek employment. Thatcher's 'Right to Buy' scheme in the UK enabled

council housing tenants to purchase their homes at relatively low cost, a popular policy that subsequent Labour governments were compelled to support which continues to the present day. According to the Local Government Association (LGA, 2023), the result is 1.2 million English households in temporary accommodation as they await social homes, and a major and growing problem of homelessness. Homelessness is of course a complex issue not solely caused by Thatcher's neoliberal housing policy, but the LGA point to the impact of the rules it imposed, which continue to constrain the possibility of rebuilding public housing.

3. Core neoliberal values allowed global markets rather than governments to set the agenda, thus freeing individuals to be autonomous; competition was seen as the wellspring of excellence, which was enacted mainly through league-tables published by monitoring agencies that sought to facilitate consumer choice. Work was re-envisioned as the solution to a wide range of social problems.

4. Initially, Hayek argued that vulnerable groups needed the protection of social and welfare safety nets because they could not compete on equal terms, but the business leaders who promoted neoliberalism rejected this moderation, reasserting the importance of deregulation and competition.

5. There is a consistently large gap between rhetoric and action that continues. Despite claims to the contrary, state provision has not been reduced. Speeches about rolling back the state and promoting small government mask the way that neoliberal states actually "impose, drive, underwrite and manage the internationalization of production and finance … often under the perverse ideological veil of promoting non-intervention" (Fine & Saad-Filho, 2017, p. 687). Yet while net state spending has not reduced, the proportion spent on social welfare and health in neoliberal economies such as the US and the UK certainly has.

6. Across the developed world, neoliberal governments have shifted moral and financial responsibility from the welfare state to the individual and their traditional family, but this is most marked in countries with the biggest distance between the richest and poorest 10% of their populations (Wilkinson & Pickett, 2010): Portugal, the US,

and the UK. Shifts in the balance of power from labour to capital have engendered the casualization and intensification of work, and limited wage growth. While Reagan (through 'Reaganomics') promoted the rhetoric that wealth accumulated at the top of societies 'trickles down' to the benefit of all, in fact as the rich get richer the poor get poorer.

7. Deprivation has been defined as not having the resource to follow the ordinary patterns of living, customs, and activities that neighbours can access. There is growing evidence that the psychological stress generated by deprivation is relative: less severe in flatter economies where most people are in the same boat, more severe in countries with the greatest wealth disparity (Wilkinson & Pickett, 2018; Kley, 2021). This is implicated in the significantly increased rates of mental illness and suicide observed in developed nations.

8. Despite the past achievements of public state provision, it is almost always and arbitrarily deemed to be inferior to private provision, often on the basis of casual or flawed studies. The citizen has been recast as a consumer whose needs and wants are best met by the free market. Neoliberalism also erodes the broader values of a public service ethos. Staff are required to satisfy consumers, which overrides their previous responsibility to determine a just course of action from a mosaic of conflicting interests.

9. Dissent is blocked institutionally in three ways. Assessment of research 'productivity' is considered a new and more sinister phase of neoliberal control that prevents blue skies thinking, and casts a shadow over small but fundamental subjects like history and philosophy (Olssen, 2016). Inspectorates drastically narrow the scope of ideas and the possibility of debate by imposing their own criteria and assessing against them, according no value to new research nor innovation (Clegg, 2008, 2017). They put enormous pressure on professionals, which resulted in the suicide of an English headteacher in 2023 when inspection of her school downgraded its previous 'Outstanding' evaluation to 'Inadequate' because of an easily fixed procedural oversight. National outrage about this resulted in a pause in inspections, but only while inspectors were trained to recognise mental health problems. The inspections then restarted, unaltered.

10. Neoliberalism retains power by 'hollowing out' organisations that are sources of challenge (Rhodes, 1994), a point that was illustrated by a neoliberal restructuring of the British Psychological Society (BPS) in 2000. Its new publishing house BPS Books had achieved worldwide influence in only 11 years by actively commissioning new titles. Despite this achievement BPS Books was closed down as uneconomic during a market-driven restructuring of the BPS focussed solely on increasing membership and income (Clegg & Lansdall-Welfare, 2020). Such hollowing out of public organisations constrains the emergence of alternatives.

11. Unrestrained competition and adverse changes in welfare regimes penalise poor and vulnerable people disproportionately, creating new patterns of life. Unparalleled prosperity for elites coexists with poverty and destitution for people who are unemployed or vulnerable. External inspection of the UK by the United Nations Council for Human Rights (2019) documented worsening deprivation, warning that a third of children being brought up in poverty carries future risks. National research confirmed this analysis. "The protective role of the state in supporting people is being reduced and realigned away from more deprived areas and communities" (Marmot et al., 2020, p. 33). Effectively, being poor has been reconstructed as a moral failing.

12. Neoliberal narratives of choice that construct the individual as an agent have been criticised by feminists as isolating; satisfactory lives are built on relationships of care that unfold over time (Power et al., 2021). Focus on agency assumes that individuals are always free to act when this is not the case, because socio-economic forces often constrain the ability to act (McNulty Norman, 2021). The new term 'Responsibilised' refers to the way that neoliberal societies hold people responsible for all their actions; the related term 'neoliberal subjectivity' refers to the way people internalise this attribution of responsibility to themselves. This absolves the state, municipality or employer of any responsibility for situations they have created.

Social problems arising from a return to levels of poverty in Britain and the United States not seen since the nineteenth century were exposed by the coronavirus pandemic. Some researchers identify signs that neoliberalism is approaching exhaustion (Jones & O'Donnell, 2019). However, all ideologies are both established and resist challenges in two ways (Honderich, 1995). First, they deploy particular kinds of explanation that express core beliefs and values, and these ideas both reflect and serve the interests of dominant parties. Second, they invert features of social reality in ways that make the social order seem natural, inevitable, or just. Saad-Filho (2021) underlined how its ideological power and shape-shifting adaptability mean that transcending neoliberalism will require considerable and co-ordinated effort on many fronts.

2   Neoliberalism and Intellectual Disability

Third-wave neoliberalism has overseen and contributed to reductions in the quality of life experienced by most people with intellectual disabilities. Tøssebro et al. (2012) reviewed evidence from Scandinavia, where initial changes expressed Nirje's (1985) radical vision before neoliberal ideology affected it. In the 1990s, individual apartments for people with intellectual disabilities in Norway were rented from local government, with a maximum of 5 such apartments to a house. Families reported feeling like they were visiting their son or daughter, not a ward, and staff reported a reduction in conflicts among residents. Subsequent dissolution of Norway's State Council on Disability and devolution of responsibility to local governments that also had responsibility for other vulnerable groups, led to service deterioration as finance cuts hit. People with intellectual disability started to be accommodated in groups that grew from an average of 3.8 in 1994 to 8.1 in 2010. When 'dedifferentiation' (no longer attending to the specifics of intellectual disability, rather incorporating them into the larger group 'people with a disability') combined with austerity financing at the local level, people with intellectual disabilities started to be housed in larger institutions with people who had other disabilities and mental health problems. There they were bullied.

Tøssebro (2016) argued that from 2000 the Scandinavian policy focus shifted from welfare to social regulation, with associated setbacks. Advocates had been naïve: they had argued successfully for high standards, but not for the structures necessary to maintain them. In the UK, geographers Power and Bartlett (2019) found older people with intellectual disabilities were living in 'deserts of care'.

The problems currently experienced by parents, staff, and people with intellectual disability in all developed countries do not arise solely from neoliberal welfare cuts. This ideology is equally problematic in Australia despite the National Disability Insurance Scheme (NDIS) (2013) being one of the most highly funded schemes in the world. It is a neoliberal policy that offers people with disabilities choice and control over the support they receive, but those with intellectual disabilities obtain significantly poorer outcomes from planners who have little if any knowledge of their needs. Making neoliberal choice central to the NDIS places unprecedented demand on parents who need time, confidence, and ability to navigate care systems and advocate for the needs of their child or adult with intellectual disability. Malbon et al. (2019) concluded that the NDIS had not just entrenched social inequalities for people with intellectual disabilities, it had widened them.

As Reinders (2000) pointed out, neoliberal attention to individual choice ducks responsibility for identifying any specific ideas that could ground service design and delivery in intellectual disability. Research into policy enthusiasm for 'Easy Read' information (Chinn, 2019) found that producing easy read materials met goals other than informing people with intellectual disability, for which there is little evidence. The process provides a significant income for charities and a high-status, sociable occupation for adults with intellectual disabilities who have few other activities open to them. Chinn argued that continuing focus on the provision of easy read materials also represent an attempt to turn people with intellectual disabilities into neoliberal consumers.

Normalisation's concern to promote patterns of life as close as possible to that followed by other citizens works well while children attend school, but less so once they leave. Young men with intellectual disability often desire what they see as a normal adult pattern of life: a wife, a job, and a car they are allowed to drive, but few of these goals are practicable for many. Individual choice cannot be the only criterion for service delivery when people long for the unachievable: the difficulties faced when this happens are shown in the example of 'Alec' that follows this section. Failure to identify and support other possible answers to the question 'what is a meaningful adult life?' leaves far too many people sitting at home known well by no-one and doing very little.

Neoliberal belief in work as the solution to social problems has resulted in significant policy efforts and research funds being allocated to preparing people with intellectual disability for a job. Beyer et al. (2016) described a two-year work experience project for 297 young people in the UK: 262 with intellectual disability and another 35 with autism. By the end, just six young people had obtained paid work, and it is possible if not probable that they all had autism rather than intellectual disability. Only a single-digit percentage of people with intellectual disability have ever held paid jobs in the UK (studies that cite bigger percentages usually turn out to refer to people with any kind of disability). Equal opportunities legislation has been one of the constraints. This prevented an Australian company from continuing to 'job-carve', that is, create customised jobs that match the skills and interests of specific individuals with intellectual disabilities (Moore et al., 2018). Employers were required to write job descriptions and publish them on the open market, available to anybody. In combination with the rapid growth of computer-driven employment practices that people with intellectual disability rarely master, this reduced the already very low proportion in paid work further. These and other constraints mean that employment rates for this group are reducing rather than improving across nations (Khayatzadeh-Mahani et al., 2020).

Finally, historians like Baistow (2001) and Marks (2015) have argued that behaviourism remains an active presence in applied psychology because its materialism and positivism chime with neoliberal principles. This is remarkable because academic psychology abandoned behaviourism just as applied psychology started to develop and promote behaviour modification and behaviour therapy. This topic is reviewed and elaborated in Chap. 4.

3   How Neoliberal Ideology Shapes Perception Unwittingly

This final section reviews data from research into the transition from school to adult services, a topic of concern that parents have raised repeatedly in different countries. It gives readers an overview of an important moment in the lives of young people with intellectual disability and their families, but also shows how little impact research can have on a dominant narrative. This section shows how neoliberal ideology appears to have resulted in a research paper being considered to prove exactly the opposite to what its data analysis had shown.

Transition research. For 25 years difficulties encountered on school-leaving (from Hanley-Maxwell et al., 1995, up to Gauthier-Boudreault et al., 2021) have been explained away by the same neoliberal trope: staff fail to communicate. As a result, many developed societies have introduced legislation or policies that require services to employ system navigators. This establishes a sequence of meetings that start years before school-leaving and are intended to improve planning and communication. Yet parents continue to complain. Our project (overviewed in Clegg et al., 2010) sought to understand what makes this moment so intractable by talking to and observing a cohort of young people as their transition progressed, interviewing parents, and interviewing staff responsible for achieving a smooth transition.

Alec was one of this cohort of 28 school-leavers with intellectual disabilities that we met over 18 months, from 12 months before he left school to 6 months afterwards, and whose leaver review meetings were recorded. Those meetings were examined using conversation analysis. Alec's intellectual disability was moderate: his verbal communication was limited to short phrases. Confidentiality commitments do not permit provision of other details, which would risk making Alec or his family identifiable.

Present at Alec's final leaver's meeting held just a few weeks before the end of his last summer term were his mother, special needs teacher, and transition co-ordinator (TC). At the start, Alec stated what he had said before, that he would like to join the police. The educational requirements were well beyond what he could attain. Young men with intellectual disability frequently hope for this, probably because children with Special Educational Need are at significantly heightened risk of being bullied 'all the time' throughout their schooling (Chatzitheochari et al., 2016). Childhood memories of overwhelming helplessness commonly underlie mental health problems experienced by adults with intellectual disability (Gallichan & George, 2016—research detailed in Chap. 4), so it is not surprising to find young people longing for an authoritative status that they imagine would protect them from harassment. The school had followed person-centred planning guidelines to give Alec some of what he wanted such as a visit to a police station, but this had not diverted him from his goal.

Participants at the meeting avoided suggesting that a job with the police may be beyond his competency. Attempts to deflect his desire for a police identity card by stating he would get an identity card if he went to college were unsuccessful. Staff avoided telling him his choice was impossible, signalling their discomfort by using increasingly oblique language that Alec did not understand: 'joining the police will be very difficult'; 'you will probably have to do something else first to get ready for that'. Eventually, after Alec reiterated that he wanted to join the police, his mother told him that he could not do that yet and would have to choose something else to do. Staff joined in the delicate rejection, which resulted in Alec leaving the meeting early. The analysis concluded as follows:

> The delicacy of the rejection is unsurprising, given that its wider implication is that Alec is unable to discern his own best interests, which is difficult territory for intellectual disability professionals in the context of the dominant discourse of self-determination and choice.... Staff are put in an impossible situation. On the one hand, they are trying to offer client-centred interactions that place the young person's competency and their right to express their desires at the heart of the transitions process. They carry responsibility for enabling the young person to take part and express choices. On the other, they are tasked with managing the fact that

a lack of competency on the part of the young people in question means that not all of these desires, however clearly expressed, can be translated into reality. *What is being asked of staff is undeliverable*; policy leads them to a position that they cannot maintain. (Pilnick et al., 2010, p. 432, emphasis added)

This article has been cited frequently. However, while we emphasised the undeliverability of the staff's task, and the stressful nature of transition co-ordination reported by staff and evidenced by high levels of staff turnover (echoed a decade later in Canada: Gauthier-Boudreault et al., 2021), this research has been cited in ways that implicitly 'responsibilises' (blames, holds responsible for) staff:

Research has shown that it can be challenging to support active adult living and self-determination in people with learning disabilities [...; Pilnick, Clegg, Murphy, & Almack, 2010]. One of the obstacles that professionals face is a lack of knowledge of what autonomy and self-determination means and how to promote it. (Witso & Kittelsaa, 2017, p. 2)

Bigby and Douglas (2020, p. 47) cited professional disempowerment as one of five barriers to self-determination: "Meetings conducted by professionals that are disempowering and obstruct rather than facilitate involvement in decision making [...; Pilnick, Clegg, Murphy, & Almack, 2010]."

How did research that explicitly challenged the responsibilisation of staff come to be cited in support of it? It appears to be an example of Honderich's (1995) argument that *ideologies are maintained by inverting aspects of social reality*. There are three possible reasons why our conclusion, that expectations placed on staff are undeliverable, was either unpalatable or unincorporable:

- As social psychology experiments on peer pressure have demonstrated repeatedly, it is difficult to challenge what everybody else seems to believe: that staff are not trying hard enough.
- There is a widely held, persistent, but under-examined belief that the main constraints on opportunity for people with intellectual disabili-

ties are the low expectations staff and parents hold for them. Developed during the challenge to institutionalisation that gained force in the 1970s, it has not been reviewed. Yet in our clinical experience in services for people in acute mental health crisis, these are most likely to be provoked by expectations that are *too high* rather than *too low*. Many parents expressed relief that this service provided assessments of cognitive and emotional development, reporting that residential staff did not listen to their estimation of their adult child's limited abilities. For example, one man admitted to an acute mental health unit after relations with staff broke down in his group home had been made to sign a three-page behavioural contract that his staff had drawn up. He could not read, and had no idea what a contract was.

- Responsibilising the staff is much easier than addressing the other, major and unspoken source of difficulty. Alec was leaving a well-resourced school staffed by well-qualified teachers who engaged him, and the options available were poorer because short-term and under-resourced. Apart from endless education that rehearses for a life that never quite happens, or hoping for a job that is an option for only a small and shrinking proportion of this group, there is little discussion of what else might comprise a fulfilling and meaningful life for adults who have intellectual disabilities.

Blaming the staff resists change and costs nothing, but fails to tackle the origin of transition problems identified for many years by many developed countries. One parent in the study described this transition as worse than the year her husband died; most of the Transition Co-ordinators felt that their job was difficult if not impossible. Half of the Transition Co-ordinators resigned during the 18 months that this research project collected data. A further two took long-term periods of sick-leave, putting further pressure on overwhelmed colleagues to pick up unfinished work. This longitudinal study showed that improving the situation was not merely a matter of staff communicating better nor simply 'raising their game', even though these continue to be the default explanations deployed by neoliberal administrations.

4 Becoming Able to See Anomalies and Imagine Possibilities That Lie Beyond Neoliberalism

Kuhn (1970) showed how scientific discoveries commence with awareness of anomaly that researchers initially struggle to notice, drawing on a psychological study to illustrate the problem. People were asked to name playing cards on brief exposure. Most cards were normal but some were anomalous, such as a red six of spades and a black four of hearts. On brief exposure all participants fitted the anomalous cards unhesitatingly into their existing cognitive scheme identifying these simply as a six of spades or a four of hearts. With longer exposures subjects began to hesitate: 'That's a six of spades, but there's something wrong with it'. Further increases in exposure resulted in more hesitation. The correct identification came quite suddenly to most people: having noticed a few anomalous cards, they were then able to identify the others without difficulty. Yet even with 40× exposure, a few people continued to express confusion and discomfort while remaining unable to make the cognitive shift.

Our culture is steeped in neoliberal assumptions that we struggle to see. We have argued they are as invisible as the air we breathe and the gravity we move through, and they are powerful: other ideas and other ways of doing things struggle to gain traction. To see what is there and start tracing a new path between impossibilities, a change of mind-set is required. Papers that unravel and name the language and assumptions behind neoliberal policies provide a start. Deconstruction of the UK's Valuing People policy by Burton and Kagan (2006) led the way, soon followed by Cumella (2008). Observations about disability from the ever-thoughtful Shakespeare (2014) are illuminating, as are the different perspectives expressed by social geographers who have not been socialised into the expected discourse, such as the following:

> It cannot be denied that many intellectually disabled people themselves *do* favour spaces with some hint of the institution about them: where they can feel a measure of security within clearly set social and spatial boundaries,

spending time alongside others who share their condition or who have a professional familiarity with it. The response should not be to reinvent 'the asylum', however, but rather to foster a myriad of geographies containing institutional, semi- and non-institutional elements. (Philo & Metzel, 2005, p. 85)

Psychologists (Pickren, 2018) and historians (Gerstle, 2022) argue that political crises in the US and the UK have provoked a moment of change that is strong enough to leave neoliberal individualism behind. The following three chapters each take one issue that recurs in intellectual disability but, like transition problems, have not been resolved by the usual way of doing things. If Deleuze is right, developing new ways to see these issues will provide a starting-point for creativity.

References

Baistow, K. (2001). Behavioural approaches and the cultivation of competence. In G. C. Bunn, A. D. Lovie, & G. D. Richards (Eds.), *Psychology in Britain* (pp. 309–329). BPS Books & Science Museum.

Beyer, S., Meek, A., & Davies, A. (2016). Supported work experience and its impact on young people with intellectual disabilities, their families and employers. *Advances in Mental health and Intellectual Disabilities, 10*(3), 207–220. https://doi.org/10.1108/AMHID-05-2014-0015

Bigby, C., & Douglas, J. (2020). Supported decision making. In R. J. Stancliffe, M. L. Wehmeyer, K. A. Shogren, & B. H. Abery (Eds.), *Choice, preference, and disability* (pp. 45–66). Springer Link. https://doi.org/10.1007/978-3-030-35683-5_3

Burton, M., & Kagan, C. (2006). Decoding valuing people. *Disability & Society, 21*, 299–313.

Chatzitheochari, S., Parsons, S., & Platt, L. (2016). Doubly disadvantaged? Bullying experiences among disabled children and young people in England. *Sociology, 50*(4), 695–713.

Chinn, D. (2019). Talking to producers of Easy Read health information for people with intellectual disability: Production practices, textual features, and imagined audiences. *Journal of Intellectual & Developmental Disability, 44*(4), 410–420. https://doi.org/10.3109/13668250.2019.1577640

Clegg, J. A. (2008). Holding services to account. *Journal of Intellectual Disability Research, 52,* 581–587.

Clegg, J. A. (2017). Does CQC encourage improvement? Commentary on "Regulating the quality of health and social care in England: Lessons for Australia. Keynote address at the 2015 Australasian Society for Intellectual Disability national conference" (Behan, Beebee & Dodds 2016). *Research and Practice in Intellectual and Developmental Disabilities, 4*(1), 98–104.

Clegg, J. A., & Lansdall-Welfare, R. (2020, July online). Psychology and neoliberalism. In *Oxford Research Encyclopaedia: Psychology: History and systems of Psychology,* Oxford University Press. https://doi.org/10.1093/acrefore/9780190236557.013.668

Clegg, J. A., Murphy, E., & Almack, K. (2010). Transition: A moment of change. In G. Grant, P. Ramcharan, M. Flynn, & M. Richardson (Eds.), *Learning disability: A life-cycle approach* (2nd ed., pp. 203–216). Open University Press/McGraw-Hill.

Cumella, S. (2008). New Public Management and public services for people with intellectual disability. *Journal of Policy and Practice in Intellectual Disability, 5,* 178–186.

Fine, B., & Saad-Filho, A. (2017). 13 things you need to know about neoliberalism. *Critical Sociology, 43*(4–5), 685–706. https://doi.org/10.1177/0896920516655387

Gallichan, D. J., & George, C. (2016). Attachment trauma and pathological mourning in adults with intellectual disabilities. In H. K. Fletcher, A. Flood, & D. J. Hare (Eds.), *Attachment in intellectual and developmental disability: A clinician's guide to practice and research* (pp. 197–222). Wiley-Blackwell.

Gauthier-Boudreault, C., Couture, M., & Gallagher, F. (2021). Obstacles to the transition to adulthood of people with severe to profound intellectual disability and potential solutions: Perspectives of professionals in one region of Quebec. *Journal of Intellectual & Developmental Disability.* https://doi.org/10.3109/13668250.2021.1873753

Gerstle, G. (2022). *The rise and fall of the Neoliberal Order.* Oxford University Press.

Hanley-Maxwell, C., Whitney-Thomas, J., & Mayfield Pogoloff, S. (1995). The second shock: A qualitative study of parents' perspectives and needs during their child's transition from school to adult life. *Journal of the Association for Persons with Severe Handicaps, 20*(1), 3–15. https://doi.org/10.1177/154079699502000102

Hayek, F. A. (1960). *The constitution of liberty.* Routledge.

Honderich, T. (1995). *The Oxford companion to philosophy*. Oxford University Press.

Jones, B., & O'Donnell, M. (2019). Conclusion: A Brexit from neoliberalism? In B. Jones & M. O'Donnell (Eds.), *Alternatives to neoliberalism: Towards equality and democracy* (pp. 245–265). Policy Press.

Khayatzadeh-Mahani, A., Wittevrongel, K., Nicholas, D. B., & Zwicker, J. D. (2020). Prioritizing barriers and solutions to improve employment for persons with developmental disabilities. *Disability and Rehabilitation, 42*(19), 2696–2706. https://doi.org/10.1080/09638288.2019.1570356

Kley, S. (2021, early online). How material deprivation impacted economic stress across European countries during the great recession. A lesson on social comparisons. Acta Sociologica, 1–20. https://doi.org/10.1177/00016993211001121

Kuhn, T. S. (1962, second edition 1970). *The structure of scientific revolutions*. University of Chicago Press.

Local Government Association. (2023). *Debate on the future of social housing*. https://www.local.gov.uk/parliament/briefings-and-responses/debate-future-social-housing-house-commons-19-april-2023

McNulty Norman, D. (2021). The responsibilised 'Agent' and other statuses. *Sociology, 1–14*. https://doi.org/10.1177/0038038520986037

Malbon, E., Carey, G., & Meltzer, A. (2019). Personalisation schemes in social care: Are they growing social and health inequalities? *BMC Public Health, 19*, 805. https://doi.org/10.1186/s12889-019-7168-4

Marks, S. (2015). Psychologists as therapists: The development of behavioural traditions in clinical psychology. In J. Hall, D. Pilgrim, & G. Turpin (Eds.), *Clinical psychology in Britain: Historical reflections* (pp. 194–207). Oxford University Press.

Marmot, M., Allen, J., Boyce, T., Goldblatt, P., & Morrison, J. (2020). *Health equity in England: The Marmot Review 10 years on*. Institute of Health Equity. http://www.instituteofhealthequity.org/resources-reports/marmot-review-10-years-on/marmot-review-10-years-on-full-report.pdf

Moore, K., McDonald, P., & Bartlett, J. (2018). Emerging trends affecting future employment opportunities for people with intellectual disability: The case of a large retail organisation. *Journal of Intellectual & Developmental Disability, 43*(3), 328–338. https://doi.org/10.3109/13668250.2017.1379250

National Disability Insurance Scheme Act. (2013). https://www.legislation.gov.au/Details/C2022C00206

Nirje, B. (1985). The basis and logic of the normalization principle. *Australian and New Zealand Journal of Developmental Disabilities, 11*(2), 65–68.

Olssen, M. (2016). Neoliberal competition in higher education today: Research, accountability and impact. *British Journal of Sociology of Education, 37*(1), 129–148.

Philo, C., & Metzel, D. S. (2005). Introduction to theme section on geographies of intellectual disability: 'Outside the participatory mainstream'? *Health & Place, 11*(2), 77–85. https://doi.org/10.1016/j.healthplace.2004.10.005

Pickren, W. (2018). Psychology in the social imaginary of neoliberalism: Critique and beyond. *Theory & Psychology, 28*(5), 575–580. https://doi.org/10.1177/0959354318799210

Pilnick, A., Clegg, J., Murphy, E., & Almack, K. (2010). Questioning the answer: Questioning style, choice and self-determination in interactions with young people with intellectual disabilities. *Sociology of Health & Illness, 32*(3), 415–436.

Power, A., & Bartlett, R. (2019). Ageing with a learning disability: Care and support in the context of austerity. *Social Science & Medicine, 231*, 55–61. https://doi.org/10.1016/j.socscimed.2018.03.028

Power, A., Coverdale, A., Croydon, A., Hall, E., Kaley, A., MacPherson, H., & Nind, M. (2021). Personalisation policy in the lives of people with learning disabilities: A call to focus on how people build their lives relationally. *Critical Social Policy, 1–21.* https://doi.org/10.1177/02610183211004534

Reinders, H. (2000). *The future of the disabled in liberal society.* University of Notre Dame Press.

Rhodes, R. (1994). The hollowing out of the state: The changing nature of the public service in Britain. *The Political Quarterly, 65*(2), 138–151.

Saad-Filho, A. (2021). *Endgame: from crisis in neoliberalism to crises of neoliberalism. Human Geography, 14*(1), 133–137. https://doi.org/10.1177/1942778620962026

Shakespeare, T. (2014). *Disability rights and wrongs revisited* (2nd ed.). Routledge.

Stedman Jones, D. (2012). *Masters of the universe: Hayek, Friedman, and the birth of neoliberal politics.* Princeton University Press.

Tøssebro, J., Bonfils, I. S., Teittinen, A., Tideman, M., Traustadóttir, R., & Vesala, H. T. (2012). Normalization fifty years beyond—Current trends in the Nordic countries. *Journal of Policy and Practice in Intellectual Disabilities, 9*(2), 134–146.

Tøssebro, J. (2016). Scandinavian disability policy: From deinstitutionalisation to non-discrimination and beyond. *ALTER, European Journal of Disability Research, 10*, 111–123.

United Nations Council for Human Rights. (2019, June 30). Visit to the United Kingdom of Great Britain and Northern Ireland: Report of the special rapporteur on extreme poverty and human rights. A/HRC/41/39/Add.1.

Wilkinson, R., & Pickett, K. (2010). *The Spirit Level*. Allen Lane.

Wilkinson, R., & Pickett, K. (2018). *The Inner Level*. Allen Lane.

Witso, A. E., & Kittelsaa, A. M. (2017). Active adult lives for persons with learning disabilities-The perspectives of professionals. *British Journal of Learning Disabilities*. https://doi.org/10.1111/bld.12207

3

A New Lens on Care Scandals

Abstract This chapter opens with a sociological analysis of the ritual way that scandals unfold: participants are identified as either sacred or profane and the situation as one that needs cleansing, which allows the public to go back to ignoring the matter. Observing an inclination to ignore matters of resource, it tracks reliance on neoliberal policies that do not constitute a resolution. Brief descriptions engender a deep appreciation of the challenges of this work and initiate the construction of a new lens focussed on supporting and sustaining direct care staff. Two such interventions within a service for adults with intellectual disabilities who can become acutely disturbed are introduced, informed respectively by systemic family therapy and European pedagogy (Heijkoop method). Readers are signposted to where they can find out more.

Keywords Intellectual disability • Scandal • Faecal smearing • Heijkoop method

Of course, the public are shocked by the maltreatment of people with intellectual disabilities. It should generate a hue and cry. Yet scandals offer a weak impetus for change: they continue to recur in wealthy as well as low- and middle-income countries, and historians of the twentieth century have observed a repeating pattern. Official neglect of intellectual disability services, with occasional critical inquiries that release short-term funds, are followed by a steady paring back of resource until the next scandal occurs.

Social scientists find a similar pattern in the twenty-first century. A 12-year follow-up (Hallam et al., 2006) of a hospital closure project found that the initial boost to funds steadily declined. Adjusted to the baseline year, weekly mean expenditure per person was £736 before hospital closure, £899 one year later, £871 five years later, but almost back to baseline by the twelfth year at £765 per person. Many apparent indicators of the benefits of community care one year after hospital closure, such as participation in the community, decreased commensurately with funding reductions across those 12 years.

This chapter examines evidence on scandalous mistreatment in institutions, and the impact of recent policy changes intended to address it. However, we start by underlining that institutions are not the only places where people with intellectual disabilities are abused. As historian Trent (1994) stated, there is a high likelihood of abuse in all settings. Meininger (2008) observed that when first encountered, intellectual disability often disturbs assumptions about what it is to be human. Without targeted efforts to improve an awkward relationship between people who are and are not intellectually disabled, every environment is likely to reproduce it. Recent research also identifies uncomfortable findings. While services seek to support parents whose baby turns out to have intellectual disability, the family has also been identified as the most likely site of abuse (Shakespeare, 2014), and the second most likely perpetrator of sexual abuse (Tomsa et al., 2021). Most of the multiple adverse childhood experiences (ACEs) that predict significant emotional difficulties in adulthood are likely to unfold in the family home. We find a way through this delicate topic very carefully in Chap. 5.

Scandals in institutions are the focus of this chapter because they are the most visible places that abuse happens, which concerned journalists bring to public attention repeatedly. That makes scandals a 'hedgehog'[1]

---

[1] Chapter 1 describes how busy professionals can fail to notice prickly hedgehogs that are repeatedly found lying alongside their path, but that attending to things that repeat is an important spur to creativity and positive change.

likely to reveal something important if we pick them up. This examination is informed by a review of the first wave of inquiries into scandals:

> Perhaps the most fundamental problem of working with the chronically ill, the very old and the severely handicapped … may be the lack of a sense of achievement …. The greatest failures of care have occurred with patients who appeared unresponsive…. Achieving a degree of order among the disturbed makes heavy demands on physical and even more, mental stamina …. *The preservation of rights is in some respects simpler to achieve than a solution to the problem of how staff can develop and retain a balanced sense of humanity.* (Martin, 1984, pp. 219–20; emphasis added)

Many of the questions raised by Martin's analysis are still pertinent, but rarely asked. Overlooking professionals and staff who work with this group to declare that all institutions should close and everybody move into the community is the preferred policy response, appearing most recently in an inquiry report in Australia (Royal Commission, 2023). Yet this fails, as the UK has amply demonstrated over the last eight years (Taylor, 2021): without consulting the people who have knowledge and experience of this complex and often difficult work, adequate alternatives are not developed and nothing changes.

1   Policy Responses to Scandals

Jacobsson and Löfmarck (2008) drew on Durkheim's argument that scandals unfold in ritual ways: they characterise participants as either sacred or profane, and the situation as one that requires cleansing. Media exposure transforms an incident into a scandal, which in turn provokes reluctant public authorities to authorise a committee of inquiry and publish its master narrative, but they only enact a small proportion of the policy changes identified. The emotional energy elicited by a scandal vanishes as soon as it appears to be resolved: the audience is reassured, relieved that they can return to chronic inattentiveness.

When there is a scandal in intellectual disability, few of the parties involved comment. Confidentiality means that professionals and care staff can make no contribution. Managers follow the advice of media experts: the way to make the press storm die down quickly is to apologise, reassure the public that lessons have been learned, and say nothing that could be considered justificatory. Journalists looking for emotional stories that might help to defend people they consider vulnerable find that only parents speak freely. Generally, parents imply that their adult child had been untroubled and was taken from their care for no reason. Such accounts are rarely probed, perhaps because—following Durkheim—inquiries into abuse by a minority of care staff position all staff as profane, all people with intellectual disabilities and their parents as innocent. That makes it difficult if not impossible to consider complex interactions between staff and residents or patients, and what impact the context of care has on both.

Research into those contexts of care (Chaplin, 2011; Chaplin et al., 2015) finds that people with intellectual disability admitted to mental health units have more severe problems than those without intellectual disability, and staff working with people who have intellectual disability and acute mental health problems endure higher levels of violence than counterparts in adult mental health. Yet distant senior managers are most likely to imagine that the people with intellectual disability in these units are like those they have met in advocacy groups (most commonly, men with Down's syndrome) who have no need of, and no experience of, acute mental health services. That leads those managers to under-estimate how serious violence can be in those services, as has often been observed (Burton & Kagan, 2006; NHS South of England, 2012; Taylor, 2021).

Halladay and Harrington (2015) compared problems in professional care environments for people with intellectual disabilities in the US and UK. In New York, widespread problems in care homes were exposed by the *New York Times* 2011–2013. In the UK, abuse at the private hospital Winterbourne View was exposed by the BBC in 2011. Their comparison showed that these US and UK scandals both followed the process outlined by Durkheim, with similar outcomes but one key difference. The main difference they found was that New York focussed on fiscal and financial problems, by creating a Justice Centre that built public law capacity to investigate and prosecute. By contrast, the UK focussed on the subject/carer relation, requiring staff to be trained in one approach, Positive Behavioural Support.

Four similar policy changes were made in both countries. (1) Managed care contracting regimes were introduced to enact a person-centred focus that politicians believed would foster better outcomes for users and tax payers. (2) Regulation and monitoring of the market were enhanced. (3) Dedifferentiation was extended: instead of specifying measures for people with intellectual disability, protections were developed and applied to all groups of people with disabilities. (4) Deinstitutionalisation was reiterated as an important answer to abuse.

Halladay and Harrington (2015) argued that scandals elicit important social interventions: by correcting societal failure to notice people with disabilities, they shift tolerance levels. Yet those first two policy responses are neither specific to this population nor to scandals: they are straightforward expressions of neoliberalism. Chapter 2 detailed what neoliberal ideas are, and how they have played out in economics and politics for so long that they have become unseeable, taken-for-granted. Thus, we should not be surprised that these authors neither questioned the appropriateness of these policy responses, nor looked for negative consequences resulting from them.

Martin's early analysis of scandals in UK hospitals for people with what were then called mental handicap and mental illness took a different approach. He sought to understand the corruption of care, asking: "How is it that institutions established to care for the sick and helpless can have allowed them to be neglected, treated with callousness and even deliberate cruelty?" (Martin, 1984, p. xi). Instead of the 'bad apple' theory enacted by the Winterbourne inquiry (Flynn, 2012), which resulted in six members of care staff going to jail while its directors were not held to account, Martin repeatedly highlighted the 'nightmarish' situations staff were left in by senior managers. "Although the brutality towards patients could not be condoned the untrained and isolated staff themselves were in a dreadful plight" (Martin, 1984, p. 81). There was also concern for ward managers. "Mrs. Z was a frightened person on a very difficult ward which was potentially quite dangerous … she was unable to deal with any of the difficulties, and difficulties arose daily" (p. 95). The situations he was examining were far more understaffed than would be found now: three staff were expected to manage 40 adults with a range of severe disorders not least life-threatening epilepsy. Yet despite contemporary

services in developed countries being smaller in size and having significantly better staff: patient ratios, the challenges of such work still means
that too few people choose to do it.

Martin (1984) concluded that while inquiries identified a few bad
apples, the matter was more complex than that: the barrel was also leak-
ing and contaminated by spores of decay, while the fruit farmer was hasty
and slapdash. When a cabinet minister asked how such deplorable conditions could have existed without them knowing about it, he was told that
negative reports had been submitted regularly to the ministry for years,
but just filed. Martin considered it no accident that most inquiries address
situations involving those who are the most severely disabled, disorganised and dysregulated. He argued the fundamental problem was that staff
lacked any sense of achievement. If any inspiring aims had been articulated at the outset, these were soon dissipated by the mundane realities
of care.

Inadequate resource is a major 'setting event'[2] for malpractice
(Martin, 1984; Trent, 1994; Thomson, 1998; Burton & Kagan, 2006).
Services for people with intellectual disabilities were less well funded
than for other comparable groups throughout the twentieth century.
After *every* inquiry Martin analysed, substantial resource was provided
to improve conditions, but such funds then get pared back until the
consequences once again became impossible to ignore. One historian
characterised care for people with intellectual disability in 1960s Britain
as follows:

> There was a belief that problems could be solved by administrative reor-
> ganization .... Questions of resources and finance, vital to any effective
> caring policy, were either evaded or relied unrealistically upon realloca-
> tion of patients from hospital to community care. (Thomson, 1998,
> pp. 294–5)

The pattern of low staff numbers boosted by short-term increases after
a scandal continued into the twenty-first century. For example, just before
the inquiry report into malpractice in the intellectual disability service at

---

[2] A prior circumstance that makes malpractice more likely.

Sutton and Merton was published, the responsible Primary Care Trust announced to the press that they had increased staff numbers by an astonishing 50%. Clegg (2008) estimated that the inquiry had cost around £2 million at that time, asking how this could possibly be justified when pre-publication action showed that the authority already knew the service was grossly understaffed.

In threadbare and understaffed settings, only a few things need to go wrong for malpractice to become a possibility. The loss of a professionally qualified manager and failure to recruit to that position is a component of many scandal inquiries, suggesting that should be a red flag that invites further scrutiny. It results in services that are not actively led, they are merely overseen by an unqualified acting manager with little job security who is not accountable to any professional organisation (this occurred in Winterbourne View: Flynn, 2012). Another red flag should be senior managers who are so preoccupied by a major system reorganisation that they do not know how poor service delivery has become. Seven reorganisations in two years resulted in no senior manager taking responsibility for the deteriorating intellectual disability service at Sutton & Merton, which the responsible board had not discussed for years (inquiry examined in Clegg, 2008). Administrative reorganisation was also identified as a contributory factor to the accidental death of Connor Sparrowhawk (Verita, 2015).

As evidenced by Halladay and Harrington (2015) but not limited to the inquiries they studied, letting scandals drive policy has resulted in the repeated application of two ideas that have dominated what is termed 'third-phase neoliberalism': the period from 1980 to the present day when neoliberal economic policies spread into all political decisions. First, although regulation and monitoring introduce no new thinking and suppress innovation, there is a surprisingly strong belief that, without further encouragement, competitive league-tables published by monitoring agencies will generate change. Second, that the only guarantors of quality are choice and personalisation. Nothing in Martin's analysis of late-twentieth century inquiries suggested that either of these would improve service delivery, and the following contemporary evidence also reveals them to be largely ineffective.

2   Understanding the Challenges of This Work

Commissioners invited to review the Winterbourne View scandal described the pressure they came under to support a small number of people differently: "Most commissioners reported that there would always be a need to access specialist individual placements in addition to local services" (NHS South England, 2012, p. 25). Their report concluded: "The level of need of most of the patients has not been acknowledged thus far" (p. 65).

Specialist services for the 40% of people with intellectual disability who experience acute mental health problems or show sustained challenges enable some people to improve radically. For others there is little if any change, which leaves staff doing mundane and at times personally difficult work with little sense of achievement. In some specialist intellectual disability services verbal and physical aggression can occur every day. Aggression may include biting ears, shoulders or breasts that require attendance at Accident and Emergency for thorough cleaning. Some people who self-harm may bang their head on floor or wall, which is distressing to witness but not straightforward to prevent. More unpalatably, there may be chronic faecal smearing that necessitates restraint while both the person and their environment are cleaned, an intervention that has provoked controversy in mental health services since Mary Barnes was left to express herself freely. In the 1960s Mary lived in Kingsley Hall, a short-lived therapeutic community led by R D Laing in London. There she was left to cover herself and its walls with art works made from her faeces (Torn, 2012). Coprophagia (eating faeces) was also a complicating feature of Sean Walton's presentation, one of the abused individuals described in the 1992 inquiry into malpractice at Moss Side special hospital (reviewed in Clegg, 2004).

Given this concatenation of difficulties, it is not surprising that intellectual disability services for people who are acutely disturbed are precarious and difficult to recruit:

Occasionally surfacing in these permissive sub-cultures were people whose personalities were more in tune with cruelty and harshness. For them the frustrations of the job were only a starting-point, and brutal and callous habits were not hard to acquire. Such people can be intimidating to colleagues…. It was not always surprising that managements, desperately short of staff, sometimes took on dubious recruits, what was less defensible was that they then took little further trouble to train or specially supervise those whose weaknesses were known from the start. (Martin, 1984, pp. 96–7)

Recruiting and retaining staff is an ongoing management challenge, and vacancies put further pressure on a stressed system. Nevertheless, as Martin pointed out and remains the case, that is no excuse for failing to actively manage all of the staff recruited. It can be even more difficult to recruit and retain managers exposed to the ever-present risk that inspectors will find them wanting. A specialist service manager in the UK reported undergoing 26 different kinds of inspections or audits per year, each entailing lengthy collation of evidence about processes of care. It kept this trusted, effective nurse away from client contact and practice leadership.

A dictum attributed to Lenin that 'Every society is only three missed meals away from chaos' could be re-written for services that support people with intellectual disability who can become distressed or disturbed. Far from any service being confident that abuse could never happen here, in our view any service for such individuals could be only three years away from an inquiry. An accidental death in the intellectual disability service at Oxford illustrates this point. An inquiry (Verita, 2015) into how Connor Sparrowhawk came to drown in the bath found that, prior to this event, the intellectual disability service was considered groundbreaking after it had received an external award. A major reorganisation that coincided with Connor's admission appears to have been associated with a rapid decline in the leadership of the service he used, resulting in poor communication both with his family and within that service. This is a reminder, if one were needed, that effective services for people with intellectual disability who can be disorganised or chaotic need not just to be developed but also to be sustained.

Just carrying out another inquiry the next time a scandal is identified will change nothing. Human systems that respond to recurring problems with 'more of the same' are problematic because they do not contain any possibility of a different outcome. Developing a rounded appreciation of the whole person and keeping that in focus requires an imaginative staff support strategy. In Sect. 4, we describe two ways of doing that. First, the limitations of the neoliberal response are identified.

3   Ineffective Neoliberal Responses

Britain has been criticised for becoming an audit society that "Invests too heavily in shallow rituals of verification at the expense of other forms of organisational intelligence" (Power, 1997, p. 123). Power warned that staff are weighed down by demands for information, which squanders resource on surveillance that should be used to support vulnerable people. Publishing inspection reports also decreases rather than increases public confidence in services, because these publicise poor rather than good practice. Powell (2019) attributed the lack of action after inquiries to a tendency to sermonise, and to inquiry reports making hundreds of recommendations with low implementability. The Commonwealth of Australia (2023) Royal Commission into Violence, Abuse, Neglect and Exploitation of People with Disability (2023) exemplifies this trend by making 222 recommendations. Not the least of the problems this will encounter is that since public services are reorganised frequently, it is rarely clear who should do what.

The following international evidence on the effects of intellectual disability policy changes implemented after inquiries is not positive:

Attempting to Reduce Restrictive Practices by Standard-Setting and Bureaucratisation

- Research that apparently shows regulation plus inspection reduces restrictive practices has been criticised for depending upon studies that use only single-subject designs, had no sampling strategy, nor ethics approval (Gaskin et al., 2013). Gaskin argued that the apparent success of regulation plus inspection was based not on research but on post-hoc decisions to write up successful interventions.

- Legislation that required staff to register restrictive practices such as restraint and isolation in Norway not only failed to decrease their use, it was associated with very significant increases. Eleven years after the introduction of legislation intended to restrict these, Sondenaa et al. (2015) examined why their recorded use had increased five-fold. They considered whether this was a real increase or just systematic recording of existing practices that had always occurred, concluding that the introduction of this legislation had to some degree acted to legitimate rather than constrain the use of restrictive practices. Supervisors had low expectations that restraint rates would decrease in the future.
- Schippers et al. (2018) found that estimates of the prevalence of coercive or restrictive practices varied widely, due to practical and definitional issues. Registering restrictive measures did not yield reliable data in the Netherlands because it was not feasible: an intervention may be restrictive or non-restrictive according to context. Moreover, while policy-makers focussed on self-determination, care staff prioritised restrictive measures that enhanced safety.
- Björne et al. (2021) found similar issues in Sweden. Compulsory registration of restrictive practices was ineffective because staff prioritised safety: they treated registration requirements as an additional bureaucratic burden rather than the intended prompt for reflection and practice change.

Personalisation and Dedifferentiation

- A meta-synthesis of research into personalisation with vulnerable elderly people published 2009–2017 found little evidence that choice over all the elements of one's service was a mechanism that improved care experiences (Fitzgerald & Kelly, 2019). This echoed earlier health research by Mol (2008) who contrasted choice and care. Care occurs between persons, is long-term not momentary and, above all, dependable. What upset patients with chronic conditions like diabetes was not lack of choice, but having been unable to access reliable care when their condition became unstable. That left them with a desolate feeling of abandonment that they recalled years later. The other significant limitation of making personalisation the funding principle is that it attaches finance solely to outcomes for the person. That provides no support for staff training and development, and makes it uneconomic to support complex individuals with multiple needs because the time required to co-ordinate their care is not funded.

- Bigby (2020) reviewed evidence on the National Disability Insurance Scheme (NDIS), a dedifferentiated personalisation policy in Australia (no longer identifying people with intellectual disabilities as a specific group, and instead including them in the broad category 'people with a disability'). Many participants with intellectual disabilities experienced problems with its implementation, because they were disadvantaged by standardised planning processes that rely on self-expressed needs. When compared to other disability groups, people with intellectual disabilities had benefitted less, had greater levels of unmet need, and those without assertive relatives were at risk of inadequate levels of support.

4   Towards a Better Approach: Add Time and Context

In Chap. 1 we outlined a Deleuzean approach to creativity, which involves throwing a conceptual net over chaos to provide a stable platform for the new. The nets he threw over a chaotic world feature duration and interaction. Deleuze theorised neither individual identity nor specific achievements, but what 'bodies in motion' (people in relationship, and their interactions with all living things and ideas in their habitat) generate over time. Consistent with that, philosopher of healthcare Mol (2008) argued that instead of neoliberal focus on choice, profit, efficiency, and consumption, words for the relational that take time should be reinstated: care, belonging, compassion. All are fundamental to adequate care for this group. However, political decisions tend to be short-term and focussed on momentary achievements that are visible.

Geographer Hall (2019) argued for a focus on the spaces and relations that constitute moments of abuse. These are more likely during economic downturns, in crowded situations, and when there is conflict over the allocation of limited resources. While it has always been difficult to recruit to health and social care settings for people with IDs, this has significantly worsened under neoliberal privatisation, which has depressed wages too far. According to the King's Fund (2023), an independent charitable organisation working to improve health and care in England, 10% of care jobs in England were vacant when the average vacancy rate across the economy was 3.4%. They identified neoliberal economic policies as the main reason for ballooning vacancies. A competitive private sector had depressed already low pay rates, which showed little progression so give no reward for staying in the job. That had exacerbated the low status of care work, leading to significant under-staffing that made the working environments even more stressful.

Governments are also chary of acknowledging that adults with intellectual disability need long-term relationships of care which, as people live longer, are increasingly necessary as a replacement for parents. Moving from very high staff turnover to sustained relationships of care is a radical change that will not be achieved easily. The 'thick' knowledge created during clinical supervision is key: how to judge what a distressed person may be feeling; how to imagine and enact a helpful response. Forensic mental health services are much further down the line in creating psychologically informed environments grounded on such transmissible knowledge. Continuity of care was also made a priority for children's mental health services in the UK. What justification can there be for its absence from services for people with intellectual disabilities who become distressed?

One major impediment to theorising longer-term relationships is that people with physical disabilities rejected the word 'care', arguing they only require 'support' to live the life they choose. As will become evident in Chap. 4, which considers emotions and the significance of attachment relationships to people with intellectual disabilities, exclusive use of the term 'support' is much less well suited to intellectual disability.

5   Seeing Scandals with Fresh Eyes

Deleuze (1968) argued that while repetition can be a spur to creativity because it highlights something we need to attend to, such creativity happens only after those examining the repeating phenomenon change themselves. Can we make ourselves so different that we become able to see the messages that lie behind the repetition of scandals, and adjust our approach accordingly?

Ways of seeing changed radically in the late twentieth century. Australian painters John Wolseley (Grishin, 2015) developed a new perspective by spending months camping in particular places supported by an aboriginal who knew the land and its rhythms well. Influenced by philosopher Deleuze he wanted to portray land as dynamic rather than static. How water and wind shift sand dunes, the kinds of bush that burn and renew, the animals that move under and on its surface as birds fly over, and the way seasons change it. In similar vein, feminist cinematographer Laura Mulvey (Another Gaze, 2018) challenged films that take a single viewpoint. She used 360° camera work that excluded editing to bring the director into the narrative. These innovations shift away from a single, man's eye gaze to offer a hybrid and multiple perspective that attends to all that is present.

Scandal inquiries seek to apportion blame, when it is more important to consider and address all the reasons that care becomes corrupted: fear, emotional exhaustion, isolation, limited skills, inadequate support, lack of specialist training, spasmodic and mainly critical attention from distant senior management:

> Current accountability practices require professionals to prove that they do well. Professionals are constantly required to praise themselves …. There is no room for doubt, self-criticism, or difficult questions. However, improvement begins with the recognition that something needs to be improved. (Mol, 2008, p. 87)

We need to find different ways of looking at and seeing the needs, experiences, and challenges for people with intellectual disabilities who are distressed or dysregulated, and the staff who, in the main, are trying to help. Failure to appreciate the stresses of their situation fuels a sense of injustice among staff, who feel they do complex arduous work for society that is neither understood nor valued. Their efforts need to be honoured, their interactional achievements acknowledged *and* they should be well trained, well supported, and have breaks that enable them to regain perspective. Without that, those who spend long periods of time with people who have intellectual disability and whose emotions can be disorganised or dysregulated are very likely to become disorientated by the experience.

The focus needs to shift from individualism and buildings (whether they are nominally 'in the community' or not) to what happens in them. This group have special needs that are difficult to recognise and interpret because their communication is compromised. A different view would start by recognising that getting their care right is difficult, and asking whether relationships are therapeutic, that is, change-promoting. Australia's NDIS contains the possibility of a separate access pathway for people with distinct and complex support needs, and these have been developed for people with psycho-social disabilities and hearing impairments. Yet the NDIS has not distinguished people with intellectual disabilities as an impairment group with distinctive issues, presumably because consumerism remains at the heart of an essentially neoliberal policy. Advocacy groups of people with intellectual disabilities mostly comprise the relatively healthy and able. They do not see themselves as different, do not want to be identified as a specific group and, far from representing those with greater needs, distance themselves from those who use wheelchairs, lack speech, or present challenges. Consequently, strategic advisors have not been appointed to represent people with intellectual disability who have acute mental health problems, nor those with the most severe and multiple disabilities whose numbers are increasing; and there is no specific access pathway. It is an opportunity missed.

There are a range of possible ways that a therapeutic environment can be fostered. One project drew on family therapy approaches in Mason's (1989) systemic intervention, which expands the way staff talk during twice-daily handovers. This approach was part of a struggling service's recovery from a disciplinary hearing, introduced by a new manager, clinical psychologist and psychiatrist, the latter two both having undergone training in family therapy (described in Clegg, 2004). Mason's new approach to conversation changes the kinds of talk that occur as staff handover from one shift to the next. It builds a therapeutic mindset by replacing an existing blame culture that tells negative stories. 'Guess what outrage Jimmy committed this morning!' was replaced by appreciative inquiries. These explored and respected ways that the leaving staff team had tried to help Jimmy, and generated new ideas about what the oncoming staff might do. It also sought positive accounts of people who had previously been distressed or dysregulated but on this occasion had had a good day. Initially, staff found the latter conversations most uncomfortable: they were wholly unaccustomed to naming positive interventions they had made that could have helped someone to turn a corner. The purpose was giving oncoming staff new strategies to employ, aiming to energise and inspire rather than depress them.

A different approach from the Netherlands, the Heijkoop method, is grounded in European pedagogy. Sessions discuss not problematic but everyday videotaped interactions, in a way that provides a reflective space where direct care and therapeutic staff could imagine and negotiate their understandings of what the person may be feeling or trying to communicate (Webb et al., 2018).

Chapter 4 examines in detail a third possible approach, which draws on attachment theory. Therapeutic interventions are informed by a collaborative attachment assessment that involves staff at all levels, and family members. This promotes understanding of how and why the person approaches other people (e.g. whether they expect to be welcomed and helped, or rejected), and the particular kinds of relationship likely to help this person develop greater emotional sensitivity and regulation.

In our view, all services for this group are potentially precarious: burnout in the face of aggression and difficult acts is an ever-present risk. It matters less what specific approach is taken, than that some therapeutic focus beyond the behavioural is identified, supported, and pursued. Those who manage and work in such services must be able to access effective training and exciting, creative supervision. Since reorganisation of services has been a setting event for neglect rather than creativity, preventative measures to avoid problems emerging during such reorganisations are also required. Whatever approach is taken, we commend a change of heart that makes incremental change, partial progress, and long-term patience more defensible.

References

Another Gaze. (2018). https://www.anothergaze.com/suddenly-woman-spectator-conversation-interview-feminism-laura-mulvey/

Bigby, C. (2020). Dedifferentiation and people with intellectual disabilities in the Australian National Disability Insurance Scheme: Bringing research, politics and policy together. *Journal of Intellectual & Developmental Disability, 45*(4), *309–319.* https://doi.org/10.3109/13668250.2020.1776852

Björne, P., Deveau, R., & Nylander, L. (2021). Passing laws is not enough to change staff practice: The case of legally mandated "incident" reporting in Sweden. *Journal of Intellectual & Developmental Disability, 46*(2), 186–196. https://doi.org/10.3109/13668250.2021.1873751

Burton, M., & Kagan, C. (2006). Decoding valuing people. *Disability & Society, 21,* 299–313.

Chaplin, R. (2011). Mental health services for people with intellectual disabilities. *Current Opinion in Psychiatry, 24*(5), 372–376. https://doi.org/10.1097/YCO.0b013e3283472524

Chaplin, R., Roach, S., Johnson, H., & Thompson, P. (2015). Inpatient Children and Adolescent Mental Health Services (CAMHS): Outcomes of young people with and without intellectual disability. *Journal of Intellect Disability Research, 59,* 995–998. https://doi.org/10.1111/jir.12148

Clegg, J. A. (2004). How can services become more ethical? In W. Lindsay, J. Taylor, & P. Sturmey (Eds.), *Offenders with developmental disabilities* (pp. 91–108). John Wiley.

Clegg, J. A. (2008). Holding services to account. *Journal of Intellectual Disability Research, 52,* 581–587.

Commonwealth of Australia (CoA). (2023, Sept. 29). Royal Commission into Violence, Abuse, Neglect and Exploitation of People with Disability : Final Report (Updated Nov. 2). https://disability.royalcommission.gov.au/publications/final-report

Deleuze, G. (1968). *Difference and repetition* (P. Patton 1994, Trans.). Continuum.

FitzGerald, M. M., & Kelly, C. (2019). Questioning "choice": A multinational metasynthesis of research on directly funded home-care programs for older people. *Health & Social Care Community, 27*, e37–e56. https://doi.org/10.1111/hsc.12646

Flynn, M. (2012). *Winterbourne view hospital: A serious case review.* http://hosted.southglos.gov.uk/wv/report.pdf

Gaskin, C., McVilly, K., & McGillivray, J. (2013). Initiatives to reduce the seclusion and restraints on people with developmental disabilities: A systematic review and quantitative synthesis. *Research in Developmental Disabilities, 34*, 3946–3961. https://doi.org/10.1016/j.ridd.2013.08.010

Grishin, S. (2015). *John Wolseley: Landmarks III.* Thames and Hudson.

Hall, E. (2019). A critical geography of disability hate crime. *Area, 51*(2), 249–256. https://doi.org/10.1111/area.12455

Halladay, P. M., & Harrington, C. (2015). Scandals of abuse: Policy responses in intellectual disabilities. *International Journal of Sociology and Social Policy, 35*(1/2), 107–124. https://doi.org/10.1108/IJSSP-12-2013-0117

Hallam, A., Beecham, J., Knapp, M., Carpenter, J., Cambridge, P., Forrester-Jones, R., Tate, A., Coolen-Schrijner, P., & Wooff, D. (2006). Service use and costs of support 12 years after leaving hospital. *Journal Applied Research in Intellectual Disabilities, 19*, 296–308.

Jacobsson, K., & Löfmarck, E. (2008). A sociology of scandal and moral transgression: The Swedish 'Nannygate' Scandal. *Acta Sociologica, 51*(3), 203–216. https://doi.org/10.1177/0001699308094166

King's Fund. (2023). Making careers in health and social care more attractive. Retrieved February 1, 2024, from https://www.kingsfund.org.uk/insight-and-analysis/briefings/making-careers-health-social-care-more-attractive. https://doi.org/10.3109/13668250.2020.1759246

Martin, J. P. (1984). *Hospitals in trouble.* Blackwell.

Mason, B. (1989). *Handing over.* Karnac.

Meininger, H. P. (2008). The order of disturbance: Theological reflections on strangeness and strangers, and the inclusion of persons with intellectual disabilities in faith communities. *Journal of Religion, Disability & Health, 12*(4), 347–364. https://doi.org/10.1080/15228960802497874

Mol, A. (2008). *The logic of care: Health and the problem of patient choice.* Routledge.

National Disability Insurance Scheme Act. (2013). https://www.legislation.gov.au/Details/C2018C00276

NHS South of England. (2012). *Report of the NHS review of commission of care and treatment at Winterbourne View.* http://www.southofengland.nhs. uk/2012/08/07/nhs-review-into-commissioning-of-care-and-treatment-at-winterbourne-view/

Powell, M. (2019). Learning from NHS inquiries: Comparing the recommendations of the Ely, Bristol and mid Staffordshire inquiries. *The Political Quarterly, 90*(2), 229–237. https://doi.org/10.1111/1467-923X.12697

Power, M. (1997). *The audit society: Rituals of verification.* Oxford University Press.

Schippers, B., Frederiks, B., Nieuwenhuijzen, M., & Schuengel, C. (2018). Reliability and feasibility of systematic registration of coercive measures in care for people with intellectual disabilities. *Journal of Policy and Practice in Intellectual Disabilities, 15*(3), 202–213. https://doi.org/10.1111/jppi.12252

Shakespeare, T. (2014). *Disability rights and wrongs revisited* (2nd ed.). Routledge.

Sondenaa, E., Dragsten, F., & Whittington, R. (2015). Practitioner explanations for the increasing use of restraint measures in the care of people with intellectual disabilities in Norway 2000–11. *Journal of Policy and Practice in Intellectual Disabilities, 12*(1), 58–63. https://doi.org/10.1111/jppi.12108

Taylor, J. (2021). Transforming care for people with intellectual disabilities and autism in England. *The Lancet.com/Psychiatry, 8,* 943–944. https://doi. org/10.1016/S2215-0366(21)00349-7

Thomson, M. (1998). *The problem of mental deficiency: Eugenics, democracy and social policy in Britain c.1870–1959.* Clarendon Press.

Tomsa, R., Gutu, S., Cojocaru, D., Gutiérrez-Bermejo, B., Flores, N., & Jenaro, C. (2021). Prevalence of sexual abuse in adults with intellectual disability: Systematic review and meta-analysis. *International Journal of Environmental Research and Public Health, 18,* 1980. https://doi.org/10.3390/ijerph18041980

Torn, A. (2012). The carnival of Kingsley Hall: The colourful case of Mary Barnes. *The Psychologist, 25*(9), 722–723.

Trent, J. W. (1994). *Inventing the feeble mind: A history of mental retardation in the US.* University of California Press.

Verita. (2015). Independent review into issues that may have contributed to the preventable death of Connor Sparrowhawk. https://www.england.nhs.uk/wp-content/uploads/2015/10/indpndnt-rev-connor-sparrowhawk.pdf

Webb, J., Pilnick, A., & Clegg, J. (2018). Imagined constructed thought: How staff interpret the behavior of patients with intellectual disabilities. *Research on Language and Social Interaction, 51*(4), 347–362. https://www.tandfon-line.com/eprint/MBkefgsAejmsW3P8x6Gq/full

4

Helping People Who Become Distressed: Attachment and Psychomotor Therapy

Abstract This chapter reviews evidence that illuminates a paradox: why do services respond behaviourally to people whose emotions become chaotic? Two emotion-focussed ways to understand and support people with intellectual disabilities are described and examined: one based on attachment theory and another relatively new approach from Europe, psychomotor therapy. Questioning the position taken by behavioural experts and echoed in policies, that any new intervention can and should be incorporated into a positive behavioural support (PBS) 'framework', the argument is made that their interiority makes them incompatible with PBS. Rather, each approach should be used to engage with and develop the emotional world of people with intellectual disabilities on its own terms.

Keywords Emotions • Intellectual disability • Attachment • Psychomotor therapy

1   Helping People with Intellectual Disability to Manage Their Chaotic Emotions[1]

Since self-harm, volatility, aggression, and violence emerge from and express strong emotions, why do anglophone countries respond to the 40% of people with intellectual disabilities who act in these ways with behavioural rather than emotional interventions? Part of the problem is the term 'challenging behaviour' that Emerson et al. (1987) coined, since framing a problem as behavioural invites a solution that is behavioural. The term's ahistorical assumption that distress and dysregulation are maintained by an immediate environment defined as unsuitable is attractive to those who baulk at any descriptor that seems to label or blame. It was of its time: after 35 years of use, it is overdue for review.

The final report of a four-year inquiry in Australia (Royal Commission into Violence, Abuse, Neglect and Exploitation of People with Disability, 2023) contains the familiar claim that positive behavioural support (PBS) is the appropriate response to people with intellectual disabilities who become distressed or disturbed. PBS is the most recent incarnation of applied behavioural analysis, which has frequently been recast to address criticisms but never fundamentally changed. PBS assumes that problematic actions are a response to the immediate environment and can be resolved by adjusting it.

A series of articles have updated PBS but the approach remains fundamentally applied behavioural analysis plus some additional contemporary elements to reassure people it is not punitive. A recent example is Gore et al.'s (2022) framework model which describes 12 components, but places behavioural approaches to learning at its centre. The text defines PBS as follows:

---

[1] This chapter is derived in part from, and significantly develops, a previously published article by Clegg and Lansdall-Welfare (2023). Helping distressed people with intellectual disability to manage their chaotic emotions. Research and Practice in Intellectual and Developmental Disabilities, 10:1, 1–15, available online open access https://doi.org/10.1080/23297018.2022.2106146

PBS has a fundamentally behavioural orientation … that provides a pragmatic solution to supporting people with learning disabilities and key people in their lives. Behavioural approaches concern scientific study and application of ways people learn and respond in relation to areas of need, life experiences, interactions with others, and aspects of their environment …. Behavioural approaches focus on the identification of variables that can be reliably evidenced in testable ways and used to both predict and influence change. (p. 18)

The PBS framework incorporates key behavioural concepts from behavioural science …. Methods and practices from applied behaviour analysis are also utilised … with regard to antecedent events, consequences and other learning processes to support behaviour and wellbeing. (p. 19)

The widely held belief that PBS is the only possible intervention is not well supported by the evidence. A comprehensive review of responses to challenging behaviour in intellectual disability (British Psychological Society & Royal College of Psychiatrists, 2015, published as a national guideline) rated the evidence for behavioural interventions as 'low' or 'very low' quality, yet the executive summary of this guideline concluded by recommending PBS for intervention in the UK. A systematic review (Simler et al., 2019) largely reiterated the conclusion that evidence in favour of PBS is weak.

More damning evidence came from a randomised controlled trial which found that training staff to use PBS did not reduce challenging behaviour (Hassiotis et al., 2018). Gore et al. (2022) argued that these staff were insufficiently trained, but a related analysis justified the study's process. Staff were given 20% more time to concentrate on these interventions, plus mentoring from an experienced behaviourist, but this was not sufficient to generate PBS plans that were any better than treatment as usual (Bosco et al., 2019). Taylor (2021) subsequently reported that there is no research to demonstrate that PBS is effective for individuals with intellectual disability who present the most serious concerns: relatively high functioning people whose aggression or violence is low frequency but high impact. Despite these critical reviews, the Australian Royal Commission (2023) repeated the earlier British policy recommendation that PBS is the required response to 'behaviours of concern' (a term no more useful than 'challenging behaviour') shown by people with intellectual disabilities. Its juggernaut presence internationally suggests that factors other than research evidence are holding this intervention in place.

Historians argue that behaviourism thrived in applied settings 50 years after it disappeared from academic psychology initially because it provided a basis for the new profession of clinical psychology, differentiating it from psychiatry; and more recently because it resonates with neoliberal ideology (Baistow, 2001; Marks, 2015). Behavioural psychology's individualism and positivism chime well with neoliberal valuing of self-management and self-reliance. Despite rejection of behaviourism by academic psychologists from Chomsky (1959) onwards, because it cannot explain complex human achievements such as language acquisition, it remains powerful in twenty-first-century clinical settings because it chimes with positivism and individualism by mirroring potent neoliberal tropes. Even though behavioural approaches are considered mechanistic, and have been used punitively and implicated in inquiries into abusive behaviour, they continue to be prioritised by the factually and morally dubious justification that 'they work':

> Behavioural approaches are more in tune with postmodern conditions than might have been predicted. Their capacity to align with changing political, economic and ethical conditions has made it possible for them to serve as useful and versatile tools in fulfilling new regulatory expectations .... Their success lies as much in their confirmation of neo-liberal shifts in attention .... Behavioural approaches have found a new political and social role; as well as creating new possibilities for citizens, they also serve to regulate them. (Baistow, 2001, p. 327)

Its recent incorporation of additional elements into a conceptual melange of incompatible ideas in the positive behavioural support framework also mirrors the shape-shifting adaptability of neoliberalism. This allows it to be presented as an adaptable solution to the many kinds of problems encountered in intellectual disability.

Behavioural interventions have shown a strong propensity to overstay their welcome in intellectual disability. Concern to support the developing emotional life of children emerged after World War II in the US and the UK, but children with intellectual disabilities were excluded from it (Toms, 2013). They continued to be brought up in institutions rather than in foster-families. There they continued to be punished for bedwetting, even though this was newly considered to express emotional distress in typically developing children that punishment would worsen.

Attending to the emotional development of children who are typically developing but not those with intellectual disabilities is a trend that continues to the present day. Underestimation of the intensity of feeling experienced and expressed by people with intellectual disabilities who become dysregulated is long-standing (Martin, 1984; Burton & Kagan, 2006; NHS South of England, 2012). While guidance on children's attachment (National Institute for Clinical Excellence guideline 26, 2015) identified stability of care as one of three major challenges that services should address, relational continuity features nowhere in policy documents on the distress and dysregulation shown by many people with intellectual disability. The high level of staff turnover in most residential services is not monitored for league-tables, nor is people experiencing frequent moves between services tracked. Morris et al. (2020) found that troubled adolescent girls with intellectual disability admitted to a forensic service had all moved through multiple placements, one as many as 13 times. Small wonder that such individuals put professionals under pressure to achieve the impossible: find them a 'forever' home. The second issue maintaining PBS appears to be that it absolves administrations from tackling major structural issues about staff recruitment and retention more adequately.

Biography is the third factor that PBS shields administrations from addressing. A growing literature reveals the impact of damage that occurs in the early years. Adverse childhood experiences (ACEs) occur much more frequently to children with intellectual disabilities than to typically developing children (Vervoort-Schel et al., 2018). A nationally representative sample of substantiated child maltreatment cases in Canada (Dion et al., 2018) found that, while children with intellectual disability are roughly 1% of the general population, they are 11% of this maltreated population. Relative to typically developing children, their abuse or neglect is more damaging because it is both more severe and more prolonged. This is significant, because maladaptive coping mechanisms developed in childhood become significant mental health problems in adults (Kezelman & Stavropoulos, 2012) not least the personality disorders that underpin extremely volatile mood swings. Ignoring the impact of negative early life-experiences draws attention away from the imperative to fund wrap-around services (Olson et al., 2021) that can reduce the incidence of ACEs.

In sum, the problems with a behavioural account of emotional dysregulation in intellectual disability is its rejection of internal experiences that are not open to observation; its rejection of historical and biological research that support alternative understandings; and its claimed ability to incorporate radically different conceptualisations based on attachment theory that are incompatible with it. A behavioural mindset has prohibited staff from using ideas and words that refer to the inner life of people with intellectual disability for decades. Having been excluded from discussion for so long, the absence of any space to record emotions or the dynamics of relationships in most pre-formatted PBS plans simply goes unnoticed.

The following two sections describe alternative therapeutic interventions that provide new ways to help people with intellectual disabilities to regulate their chaotic emotions through the support of parents and staff.

2   Attachment Theory

Naming a theory about the subtle connections between human beings with a familiar word 'attachment' makes people believe they know what it means, which is and is not true. Its use in everyday language correctly evokes familiar moments when a young child who feels under threat from a strange person or situation hides behind the legs of an adult they trust, and sometimes clings to them. Yet when attachment is raised in clinical settings more used to behavioural language, staff sometimes say what is not true: that when adults with intellectual disabilities display intense and prolonged clinging to a selected member of staff, the issue is not attachment but rather that they are 'too attached'. Effortful learning is required before people can understand that excessive clinging is very much an aspect of insecure attachment that benefits from being understood and responded to using those ideas.

An apparently trivial demonstration of the continuing dominance of behaviourism into the very language of intellectual disability is recent emergence of the new term 'attachment behaviour' (e.g. Mullen, 2018). There are no such definitive behaviours. Secure and insecure attachment relational bonds are inferred. Entry into this world of meaning for researchers usually requires attendance at intensive two-week training courses. Teaching and detailed analysis of videos and transcripts are required before raters can recognise and differentiate between different kinds of attachment reliably. Much of what people do is not significant, while easily missed moments can be significant even though fleeting. The way people talk is generally more influential than what they say. Ascription of a type of attachment only emerges after an array of different kinds of indicators has been identified and composited into a coherent picture.

There is also a political dimension. Bowlby developed attachment theory from 1950 onwards. Claims it is a universal have given way to acceptance that this was of its time, a colonialising discourse that should be abandoned. Bowlby's (1951) earliest description of attachment attributed difficulties to 'maternal deprivation', which soon evoked challenges and criticism for resisting women's emancipation, not least their ability to work. The growing feminist movement (Clarke & Clarke, 1976; Bauman, 1994) kept their critique focussed on the myth of maternal deprivation despite having access to Bowlby's (1969) revised theory. This moved beyond previous hints of 'mother blaming' to address the sequelae of loss and separation in their own terms.

A different kind of political hazard arises from the different characteristics of attachment observed in typically developing children and adults. Since adults with intellectual disabilities show developmental characteristics of both children and adults, attachment researchers have had to engage with the legacy of Wolfensberger's (1972) normalising discourse, which condemned the ascription of childish characteristics to adults with intellectual disability. This critique has softened over time as the cruelty of removing toys from adults with profound intellectual disabilities but replacing them with nothing was revealed, and the helpfulness and relevance of developmental approaches have become more evident.

Recent research in intellectual disability has refreshed attachment as an alternative to behaviourism that can inform intervention for people who become distressed. Some 42% of children with intellectual disability referred to mental health services in the Netherlands had disordered attachments (Giltaij et al., 2013). Researchers from the leading Dutch group (Schuengel et al., 2016) observed that children with intellectual disability have more need of attachment relationships, but unfortunately disorders of attachment occur relatively frequently in this group.

A key finding in support of an attachment perspective is that the emotional development of people with intellectual disabilities lags significantly behind their cognitive development, and their level of emotional rather than cognitive development has been found to predict degree of dysregulation (Sappok et al., 2014). That gives grounds for optimism: despite brain impairment, it should be possible to bring the level of emotional development of most people at least up to their level of cognitive development. A European co-operative of researchers has built an impressive body of work about this over some 15 years, culminating in a comprehensive account (Sappok et al., 2022). This book summarises research by them and others, and explains the development and validation of the Scale of Emotional Development—Short (SED-S), a formative assessment that informs and shares intervention by professionals, care staff and parents. The book ends with detailed examples of how these assessment insights inform effective practice.

In addition to research from Europe, a parallel body of work is emerging from the UK and the US: Gallichan and George (2016); Gallichan and George (2018). This research validates a relatively new attachment assessment that is appropriate for people with mild intellectual disabilities: the Adult Attachment Projective Picture System. This invites people to tell a story based on pictures they are shown, which start with neutral events then move onto situations that evoke attachment feelings. Early findings are that overwhelming memories of feeling helpless, and of loss and bereavement, play a significant role in the distress felt by people with intellectual disabilities.

Play therapy used with children who have mental health problems is also beginning to be used to help children with intellectual disabilities and their mothers to engage. Hofstra et al. (2023) researched its impact for children with mild-borderline intellectual disabilities who had a disturbed attachment to their mothers. The sample of 28 pairs contained 16 who dropped out of treatment, which underlines how difficult it can be to change the way people relate. This is most likely related to them not having had their attachment needs met as children. The 12 pairs who stayed in the study showed significant improvements in their interactional quality.

This is a strong international body of research into attachment and intellectual disability. It is a shame that this evidence struggles to gain traction on policy and practice outside Europe. It makes no claim to apply to everybody. Sometimes, approaching distress from an entirely different route is more helpful.

3   Psychomotor Therapy

Psychomotor therapy opens a new path to turbulent emotions by starting with the body. The European profession of psychomotor therapy blends aspects of physiotherapy and psychological therapy. It considers possible meanings of the clumsiness, odd postures, hyperactivity, tics, and distorted body image that frequently accompany neurodevelopmental disorders. Psychomotor therapy is grounded in activity: a recent conference of psychomotor therapists[2] mixed formal presentations in a lecture hall with interactive, movement-based workshops. These were held in spaces without chairs to allow people to move around engaging with one another: interactions had much in common with constructive negotiations between people that are fundamental to family therapy training and practice.

Psychomotor therapy is welcomed by many people with intellectual disabilities who become distressed or dysregulated, perhaps because it is

---

[2] *The treatment of sexual trauma and anger relation problems,* November 2023, Windesheim University, Zwolle, the Netherlands.

active and they find it unthreatening. It enables people to reflect on the relationship between experiences and feelings by using different activities that focus on noticing bodily responses rather than events or emotions. In our pilot study (Kay et al., 2016), its basis in physical activity rather than talking or table-top activities was welcomed by many of the residents on an acute mental health unit. It was also found to be feasible and to enrich clinical formulations, so presents an alternative way to understand and manage strong feelings.

Rather than regarding sensations to be the result of thought, psychomotor therapists start by inviting people to notice and comment on their embodied life. Intervention combines body awareness exercises with physical activity to stimulate reflection that can improve mental health. Research with people who have intellectual disabilities (Bellemans et al., 2018) identified the importance of developing 'interoceptive awareness'. Therapy directs their attention to changes in their body in order to distinguish between and manage different feelings.

Kay et al. (2016) found a striking degree of bodily neglect during assessments of adults with intellectual disabilities and mental health problems or considered challenging who had been admitted to a short-term assessment and treatment unit. Some were invited to walk on a treadmill and the speed gradually increased. They started to perspire and breathe more deeply, but when asked if they noticed anything changing in their body replied 'no' even when directed to attend to those specific aspects. Another part of the assessment invited them to lie prone with eyes closed, then a quoit was placed on their body in different places. They were asked to point to it as soon as they felt its placement. Some people missed over half of these events. The idea that they were neglecting available body feedback was confirmed by various games that enhanced their sensitivity to change within a few sessions.

Activities were interspersed with reflective exercises, such as inviting the person to look at themselves in a full-length mirror, then describe what they saw and how they felt about their body. One woman who was not markedly dysmorphic ran out of the room as soon as the mirror was brought out. Once settled by familiar staff and reassured that the mirror had been removed, she explained that it had been years since she felt able to look in a mirror. She went on to reveal a profound sense of self-disgust that staff who thought they knew her well had not previously understood.

Psychomotor therapy explained and helped to address unusual jumping behaviour of a young woman admitted to this unit following the breakdown of her family relationships. Having been living in an overcrowded house where she shared a small bedroom with two other people, when shown into her own room on the unit she looked at it in wonder and stayed there for almost a month, mostly under the duvet (hypoarousal). Once she started to get up and move around, this woman drew a peer into a jumping game on her bed which they used as a trampoline. They jumped long and hard for considerable periods of time, apparently unable to stop (hyper-arousal) without considerable intervention from staff. She also jumped when alone in the middle of the night.

This jumping was understood to be an inappropriate response to an uncomfortable level of arousal. Following advice from the psychomotor therapist, staff worked with her to regulate her level of arousal through joint action. They encouraged her to ride on a static bike, then accompanied her as they walked around the unit, then sat with her as they had a warm drink, which changed her state of arousal steadily and allowed her to return to bed and sleep. Unfortunately, the service to which she was discharged ignored explanations that her jumping was an inappropriate attempt to bring her arousal to a more comfortable level, which required co-regulation by staff. They treated her jumping as a challenging behaviour, analysing it for precipitants and reinforcers. The jumping escalated to such a degree that co-residents complained about noise in the middle of the night, she broke her bed, and the placement soon broke down.

That experience demonstrates the hurdles to innovation presented by an ossified environment. Psychomotor therapy has become well established in Europe with children and adults who have mental health problems, particularly anorexia nervosa and schizophrenia. The approach is well suited to assessing and treating people with intellectual disability who find it difficult both to express themselves verbally and to interpret bodily arousal appropriately (McDonnell et al., 2015). Yet services struggle to set aside behavioural assumptions and use new ways to understand and help their clients.

The feasibility study outlined above (Kay et al., 2016) used an assessment developed for children that was translated for the study by Emck, its author. The most commonly issues identified were participation and enjoyment (*n* = 6), self-control (*n* = 6), and body acceptance (*n* = 5). Body acceptance was a significant issue for three of the four people diagnosed with autism. A comparison of incidents prior to assessment and therapy, and just after each session, provided a check on whether psychomotor assessment or therapy increased the risk of aggression afterwards: it did not.

The English-language evidence base of psychomotor assessment and therapy with people who have intellectual disabilities is limited but growing rapidly. Research was published initially by the *Journal of Intellectual and Developmental Disability*, broadening out recently into the *Journal of Policy and Practice in Intellectual Disability* and *Research in Developmental Disability*. A recent psychomotor assessment of people with intellectual disabilities has been developed to underpin treatment of anger-related interoceptive awareness (Bellemans et al., 2018). Other psychomotor publications address sexual abuse in ID: an interview-based assessment (The Body Experience Questionnaire, Smit et al., 2022) and its treatment (Smit, 2023).

4   Conclusion

Complex combinations of social and embodied difficulties that affect people with intellectual disability make it an extremely heterogeneous group. It is very unlikely that one approach could work with everybody, but the claim that PBS provides a broad and unifying framework makes it attractive. It has held sway for three decades, squeezing out much-needed creativity and innovation which attracts little attention or funds. Being widely recognised and relatively cheap to implement has probably influenced the longevity and popularity of PBS with policy-makers, whose monitoring agencies require simple answers that can be assessed by inspectors with limited expertise,

This chapter has made the case for shifting focus from behaviour to emotions, providing two distinct ways that this can be assessed and brought into practice. However, without creating their own unique conceptual environment that allows them to exist, they are likely to disappear just as family therapy has disappeared from intellectual disability (described in Chap. 1). PBS keeps going because it chimes with neoliberalism, and intellectual disability service systems have made training and policy investments in it. In 'Negotiations' (Deleuze, 1990), a compilation of conversations held over 20 years, he drew on Kafka's *The Trial* to remind us that endless postponements are a control mechanism. He encourages us instead to be active now: to value the creative energy we and those we support experience as we all become different:

- "You have to see creation as tracing a path between impossibilities… it's by banging your head on a wall that you find a way through." (Deleuze, 1990, p. 133)
- "I think it's stupid summing things up …. It's not beginnings and ends that matter but middles …. That's where everything unfolds." (p. 161)
- "It definitely makes sense to look at the various ways individuals and groups constitute themselves … what counts in such processes is the extent to which, as they take shape, they elude both established form of knowledge and the dominant forms of power …. You precipitate events, however inconspicuous, that elude control." (p. 176)

Policy changes that seemed impossible have occurred suddenly in intellectual disability when an accumulation of criticism and awareness of tensions create a watershed. For those who are willing to take a different look at the issues that affect a significant proportion of this population, by replacing a behavioural with an emotional lens, Attachment and Psychomotor Therapy provide viable alternatives. As exciting new researchers allow these new concepts to gain momentum and generate a new *plane of immanence* on which they can rest (make sense), many more people with intellectual disabilities troubled by chaotic emotions will get the emotional support they need.

References

Baistow, K. (2001). Behavioural approaches and the cultivation of competence. In G. C. Bunn, A. D. Lovie, & G. D. Richards (Eds.), *Psychology in Britain: Historical essays and personal reflections* (pp. 309–329). British Psychological Society Books.

Bauman, E. (1994). *Deconstructing developmental psychology*. Routledge.

Bellemans, T., Didden, R., Visser, R., Schaafsma, D., Totsika, V., & van Busschbach, J. T. (2018). Psychomotor therapy for anger and aggression in mild intellectual disability or borderline intellectual functioning: An Intervention Mapping approach. *Body, Movement and Dance in Psychotherapy, 13*(4), 234–250. https://doi.org/10.1080/17432979.2018.1471006

Bosco, A., Paulauskaite, L., Hall, I., Crabtree, J., Soni, S., et al. (2019). Process evaluation of a randomised controlled trial of PBS-based staff training for challenging behaviour in adults with intellectual disability. *PLOS ONE, 14*(8), e0221507. https://doi.org/10.1371/journal.pone.0221507

Bowlby, J. (1951). Maternal care and mental health. *Bulletin of the World Health Organization, 3*, 355–533.

Bowlby, J. (1969). *Attachment and loss, Vol. 1: Attachment*. Basic Books.

British Psychological Society & Royal College of Psychiatrists. (2015). *Challenging behaviour and learning disabilities: Prevention and interventions for people with learning disabilities whose behaviour challenges (NICE guideline 11)*. National Institute for Health and Care Excellence.

Burton, M., & Kagan, C. (2006). Decoding valuing people. *Disability and Society, 21*, 299–313.

Chomsky, N. (1959). A review of B. F. Skinner's *Verbal Behavior*. *Language, 35*(1), 26–58.

Clarke, A. M., & Clarke, A. D. B. (1976). The formative years? In A. M. Clarke & A. D. B. Clarke (Eds.), *Early experience: Myth and evidence* (pp. 3–24). Open Books Publishing.

Deleuze, G. (1990). *Negotiations* (M. Joughin, 1995, Trans.). Columbia University Press.

Dion, J., Paquette, G., Tremblay, K.-N., Collin-Vézina, D., & Chabot, M. (2018). Child maltreatment among children with intellectual disability in the Canadian Incidence Study. *Journal of Intellectual & Developmental Disability, 123*(2), 176–188. https://doi.org/10.1352/1944-7558-123.2.176

Emerson, E., Toogood, A., Mansell, J., Barrett, S., Bell, C., Cummings, R., & McCool, C. (1987). Challenging behaviour and community services: 1.

Introduction and overview. *British Journal Learning Disabilities, 15*(4), 166–169. https://doi.org/10.1111/j.1468-3156.1987.tb00430.x

Gallichan, D. J., & George, C. (2016). Attachment trauma and pathological mourning in adults with intellectual disabilities. In H. K. Fletcher, A. Flood, & D. J. Hare (Eds.), *Attachment in intellectual and developmental disability: A clinician's guide to practice and research* (pp. 197–222). Wiley-Blackwell.

Gallichan, D. J., & George, C. (2018). The adult attachment projective picture system: A pilot study of inter-rater reliability and face validity with adults with intellectual disabilities. *Advances in Mental Health and Intellectual Disabilities, 12*(2), 57–66. https://doi.org/10.1108/AMHID-11-2017-0036

Giltaij, H., Sterkenburg, P., & Schuengel, C. (2013). Psychiatric diagnostic screening of social maladaptive behaviour in children with mild intellectual disability: Differentiating disordered attachment and pervasive developmental disorder behaviour. *Journal of Intellectual Disability Research, 59*(2), 138–149. https://doi.org/10.1111/jir.12079

Gore, N., et al. (2022). Positive behavioural support in the UK: A state of the nation report. *International Journal of Positive Behavioural Support, 12*(Suppl. 1), 1–46.

Hassiotis, A., Poppe, M., Strydom, A., Vickerstaff, V., Hall, I. S., Crabtree, J., Omar, R., King, M., Hunter, R., Biswas, A., Cooper, V., Howie, W., & Crawford, M. J. (2018). Clinical outcomes of staff training in positive behaviour support to reduce challenging behaviour in adults with intellectual disability. *The British Journal of Psychiatry, 212*, 161–168. https://doi.org/10.1192/bjp.2017.34

Hofstra, E., Kasius, M. C., & Vermeiren, R. R. J. M. (2023). Treating children with disturbed attachment and an intellectual disability: Effectiveness of theraplay-based treatment. *International Journal of Play Therapy, 32*(4), 230–242. https://doi.org/10.1037/pla0000204

Kay, J., Clegg, J. A., Emck, C., & Standen, P. J. (2016). The feasibility of psychomotor therapy in acute mental health services for adults with intellectual disability. *Journal Intellectual and Developmental Disabilities, 41*(1), 54–60. https://doi.org/10.3109/13668250.2015.1094037

Kezelman & Stavropoulos. (2012). Practice guidelines for treatment of complex trauma and trauma informed care and service delivery. *Adults Surviving Child Abuse.* https://www.blueknot.org.au/resources/Publications/Practice-Guidelines

Marks, S. (2015). Psychologists as therapists: The development of behavioural traditions n clinical psychology. In J. Hall, d. Pilgrim, & G. Turpin (Eds.),

Clinical psychology in Britain: Historical perspectives (pp. 194–207). The British Psychological Society.

Martin, J. P. (1984). *Hospitals in trouble.* Blackwell.

McDonnell, A., McCreadie, M., Mills, R., Deveau, R., Anker, R., & Hayden, J. (2015). The role of physiological arousal in the management of challenging behaviours in individuals with autistic spectrum disorders. *Research in Developmental Disabilities, 36,* 311–322. https://doi.org/10.1016/j. ridd.2014.09.012

Morris, D. J., Webb, E. L., Parmar, E., Trundle, G., & McLean, A. (2020). Troubled beginnings: The adverse childhood experiences and placement histories of a detained adolescent population with developmental disorders. *Advances in Mental Health and Intellectual Disabilities, 14*(6), 181–197. https://doi.org/10.1108/AMHID-01-2020-0003

Mullen, G. (2018). Intellectual disability and attachment theory among adults: An early systematic review. *Journal of Intellectual & Developmental Disability, 43*(3), 252–263. https://doi.org/10.3109/13668250.2017.1410769

NHS South of England. (2012). Report of the NHS review of commission of care and treatment at Winterbourne View. http://www.southofengland.nhs. uk/2012/08/07/nhs-review-into-commissioning-of-care-and-treatment-at-winterbourne-view/

NICE guideline 26. (2015). *Children's attachment: Attachment in children and young people who are adopted from care, in care or at high risk of going into care.* National Institute for Health and Care Excellence. www.nice.org.uk/guidance/ng26

Olson, J. R., Benjamin, P. H., Azman, A. A., Kellogg, M. A., Pullmann, M. D., Suter, J. C., & Bruns, E. J. (2021). Systematic review and meta-analysis: Effectiveness of wraparound care coordination for children and adolescents. *Journal of the American Academy of Child and Adolescent Psychiatry, 60*(11), 1353–1366.

Royal Commission into Violence, Abuse, Neglect and Exploitation of People with Disability: Final report. (2023). ISBN 978-0-6457941-5-1 (print); ISBN 978-0-6457941-6-8 (online).

Sappok, T., Budczies, J., Dziobek, I., et al. (2014). The missing link: Delayed emotional development predicts challenging behavior in adults with intellectual disability. *Journal of Autism and Developmental Disorders, 44,* 786–800. https://doi.org/10.1007/s10803-013-1933-5

Sappok, T., Zepperitz, S., & Hudson, M. (2022). *Meeting emotional needs in intellectual disability: The developmental approach.* Hogrefe.

Schuengel, C., Clegg, J., de Schipper, J., & Clasien, K. S. (2016). Adult attachment and care staff functioning. In H. Fletcher, A. Flood, & D. Hare (Eds.), *Attachment in intellectual and developmental disability: A clinician's guide to practice and research* (pp. 151–171). John Wiley.

Simler, A., Davies, B., & Hartwright, C. (2019). *How effective is positive behavioural support for adult service users? A systematic review.* DClinPsy Thesis, Cardiff University, UK.

Smit, M., Scheffers, M., Emck, C., et al. (2022). The body experience Questionnaire for adults with mild intellectual disability or borderline intellectual functioning. *Journal Intellectual and Developmental Disability, 47*(2), 141–151. https://doi.org/10.3109/13668250.2021.1929870

Smit, M. J. (2023). *Sexual abuse in individuals with intellectual disability: A psychomotor perspective.* Thesis Vrije Universiteit, Amsterdam. https://doi.org/10.5463/thesis.323

Taylor, J. (2021). Positive behavioural support for people with intellectual disabilities in forensic settings: A case of the emperor's new clothes? *International Journal of Positive Behavioural Support, 11*(1), 7–14.

Toms, J. (2013). *Mental Hygiene and psychiatry in modern Britain.* Palgrave Macmillan.

Vervoort-Schel, J., Mercera, G., Wissink, I., Mink, E., van der Helm, P., Lindauer, R., & Moonen, X. (2018). Adverse childhood experiences in children with intellectual disabilities: An exploratory case-file study in Dutch residential care. *International Journal of Environmental Research and Public Health, 15*(10). https://doi.org/10.3390/ijerph15102136

Wolfensberger, W. (1972). *The principle of normalisation in human services.* National institute on Mental Retardation.

5

Reshaping the Way Parents and Services Relate

Abstract Neoliberal individualism emphasises that adults with intellectual disabilities are adults first, which sidelines parents even when they provide 24-hour care and support. The chapter opens by examining narratives from research and practice that reveal different perspectives between services and parents of adults, and suggest strategies to negotiate them. It examines a dilemma for services, that they exist to help parents but also to check whether they might be abusive or damaging. One way to address this constructively is to find topics that relate to both dimensions. Poverty is proposed as one phenomenon that illuminates both aspects. While recognising that abuse does not only occur in impoverished families, and that most poor families are not abusive, future research into intellectual disability should nevertheless make it possible to understand and address poverty. Projects should be funded to recruit representative samples, and editors encouraged to value if not require them. Tools to improve the relationship between parents and services are reviewed. The potential significance of communities of solidarity are explored, as recent research suggests that these are more important than inserting the 'voice' of intellectual disability into government and policy.

Keywords Intellectual disability • Power Threat Meaning framework •
poverty • Enabling Environments

The relationship between parents and services is the prickliest hedgehog, since giving and receiving help is rarely without tension. Fifty years ago, Peter Mittler, then newly appointed Director of the Hester Adrian Research Centre at the University of Manchester, sought to tackle the issue of parents and services regarding one another as the enemy. Since then, child services have adopted many helpful strategies for engaging with parents, where family therapy approaches thrive. For a while it seemed that family therapy might blossom in adult services, but this dwindled to nothing in one generation (details in Chap. 1). Focus on promoting autonomy means that interactions between parents of adults with intellectual disability and service providers are examined rarely. Most research addresses the perspective of one or other party.

1   What Complicates the Parent-Services Interface

Rich accounts of parenting someone with intellectual disability have been written by mothers who are also academics, such as philosopher Feder Kittay (1999). Solomon (2014) underlined the awe-inspiring achievements of couples who parent a 'different' child. Such positive accounts have only occasionally been challenged by mothers who point out normalisation's ideological underside. Saetersdal (1997) argued that it had made suffering an ugly word: the disabled and their families were being forced into a 'Pollyanna' culture that only focussed on the positive and upbeat. Voysey's grounded theory research with new mothers as they made sense of their situation also observed pressure on them to be positive. These mothers were socialised into saying the experience had revealed new meaning to them after they found no audience for their distress. Subsequently republished as a sociology classic, the author's new preface argued that little had changed (Voysey-Paun, 2017). Critical disability studies researcher Ryan (2021) has given a more recent account.

The significant toll of parenting a child with a disability is overlooked when the well-being of the individual is the only focus. Family therapists who seek the perspective of all family members also frequently discover unrecognised ill-health in parents of any age (Baum & Lyngaard, 2006). Population studies find that the mental and physical health of parents over 60 still caring for adult children with intellectual disability is significantly poorer than that of peers, and declines further in their 70s (Namkung et al., 2018). Yet concerns about deteriorating services mean that many continue to care long after this has ceased to be in their best interests (Miettinen, 2012).

Early parent studies found that support services were insensitive to the life course dimension of their lives, offering only respite care (Todd & Shearn, 1996); and that mothers feel under constant scrutiny from services (Todd & Jones, 2003). While parents choose to accept their situation with dignity, it is a burdensome life. Ryan's (2021) long list of unwelcome administrative tasks that fall to parents in the UK echoed concerns that Dreyfus and Dowse (2020) found weighing down parents in Australia. Not only making and managing relationships with many different services and professionals, but also collecting aids and appliances from soulless buildings, educating themselves and others, and seeking support while resisting poor service delivery.

In Chap. 2 we described a longitudinal research study into the transition from school carried out with a cohort of 28 school-leavers. One of the papers from this study (Clegg et al., 2017) examined the way decisions with and for these young people with moderate to severe intellectual disabilities were made and accounted for. Below are a few details from that research concerning one complex young woman 'Lottie', to help readers appreciate the problems that can arise when a verbally able but volatile young woman says different things in different circumstances to different people. As previously indicated, confidentiality means that we cannot give a fully rounded account of this young woman nor her mother. The following outline sketches her situation to illuminate the kinds of tensions that can develop between a mother and services:

> Lottie had complex epilepsy from early childhood that compromised her ability to reason and recall, which became unstable during the transition

out of school as sometimes happens during adolescence as bodies change. However, denying that epilepsy caused her any difficulties in remembering or reasoning, Lottie would refuse to discuss it or any other difficulties. She walked out of situations where these were raised, including during appointments with her neurologist. The outcome of Lottie's transition from school was a residential college placement that she and others evaluated variably. Its distance meant that her transition worker only saw her during the holidays while at home, where she consistently maintained that she did not want to return. However, her mother evaluated the college placement positively, emphasising that on returning there Lottie would walk in willingly, go straight to her room to drop her things and then go to the kitchen to make tea and chat to staff and fellow residents. Her mother pointed out that, like many adolescents, Lottie would prefer to be at home doing nothing but that would not engender a decent life. Learning independent living skills at college that she would not allow her mother to teach her could be life-changing. Given her refusal to remain in other settings, Lottie's demeanour at the college made her mother believe it was an appropriate and successful placement. She accepted that the return of seizures upset Lottie, and constrained her options as the college considered she was currently not safe to go out alone. Getting on top of those was the real issue.

While discourses of choice treat the self-determination of people with intellectual disabilities as a simple matter of parents and transition workers listening to these young people and facilitating what they want, this was rarely the case across this cohort of 28 young people. Few of the 'choices' made on school-leaving could be considered informed nor made by young people with the capacity to make them. Wishing that services would adopt a more rounded view of them and their lives, many parents repeated the familiar trope: *You only get what you fight for.*

Other parents (Charnock, 2014) have complained about services that encourage desires in young men that they have to disappoint. A school for young people with intellectual disabilities allowed them to drive an old car around their large car park; being off-road, this is legal in the UK without a provisional licence. Delighting the pupils but giving their parents a headache, it fuelled their sons' demand for driving lessons when driving was clearly beyond them: their decision-making was too slow, their breadth of thinking too narrow. In similar vein, another project heard that Emily had to disappoint Jason's unrealistic hope of running his own media business:

> "You cannot explain to him…. In some very, very basic ways he's clueless." Emily …. told me mournfully, "The primary job of most parents is to make their kids think they can do anything; my primary job is to take him down. Reduced to a sentence it's 'You're not smart enough to do what you want to do'. Do you know how much I hate having to say that?" (Solomon, 2014, p. 174)

The way a school-leaver's meeting stalled when Alec repeated his long-standing wish to join the police was outlined earlier (Chap. 2). This put the professionals into an impossible situation because, while the educational qualifications required for the police were well beyond Alec's reach, the moral imperative is never to snuff out hope (Pilnick et al., 2010). Like Emily, it was Alec's mother who was left to rescue the situation. She told him he could not join the police now, he would have to choose another way to spend his time after leaving school—at which point Alec left the meeting. With just a few weeks until he left school, his mother and staff had to arrange some activity for him. This exchange has been cited by others as disempowering. Apparently confident they would have involved Alec successfully had they been there, critics give no details of how they would have achieved that.

The views of parents and adults with intellectual disability who live with them will not always coincide: parents are trying to be realistic, to balance the needs of all family members, and to manage their own jobs and lives (Williams & Robinson, 2001). Yet service-providers rarely acknowledge such tensions in meetings that focus exclusively on the young person with intellectual disability. This leaves parents in a delicate position, having to lay off discussion of their lives with opening remarks such as "Just being selfish for my own sake" (Pilnick et al., 2011). Talk about the limitations imposed by intellectual disability is also suppressed as family members act to protect one another from the distress it might evoke, a process that professionals mirror (Pote et al., 2011).

On the other side of this relationship, professionals and service providers often recognise what parents need, but do not always have it in their toolbox. Resource for this relatively small and overlooked population is almost always capped, with occasional short-term boosts that are then reeled in. Services are set up to deliver problem-solving interventions like medication or specific therapies. However, it is not always clear what brings parents to the door of services: discovering that requires time and trust-building. Managers may be expected to demonstrate how intervention leads to change, but many parents are not in a position to embrace change. What many want is access to a professional who knows them and their adult with intellectual disability, and holds different kinds of knowledge. Losing the long-term, trusted support of specialist teachers as their young person with profound and multiple intellectual disabilities moved into adulthood led one parent to say that it felt like being cast off in a very small boat into a very large ocean (King, 2023). They want somebody who will journey with them as they address multiple issues, and alert them to new possibilities as they arise.

Recent evidence has further complicated the relationship between parents and services. Research from different countries reviewed in Chap. 4 finds the adverse childhood experiences that underlie significant mental health problems in adulthood happen to children with intellectual disabilities much more frequently than to children who are typically developing. Even though media and—probably as a consequence—policy attention focuses on residential staff as potential abusers (reviewed in Chap. 3), extensive systematic reviews that Shakespeare led on behalf of the World Health Organisation led him to conclude: "Family members are the commonest perpetrator of abuse and violence" (2014, p. 228). Family members have also been identified as the second most likely perpetrators of sexual abuse, peers being the first, service staff a long way third (Tomsa et al., 2021). These kinds of tensions make negotiating a collaborative relationship between services and parents of adults who have intellectual disability essential but delicate. Differences in position must be negotiated and compromises accepted.

The previous two examples explored some frustrations parents have with services. The following vignette is a composite of people and situations we have supported, offered to provide insight into the kinds of complex issues that services experience:

'Dave' had a settled and satisfactory social life when he was well. However, repeatedly he needed to be admitted to an acute mental health unit to stabilise his diabetes, because becoming hypo-glycaemic made him dangerously confused. He did not understand how to manage diabetes, lived in his own flat, and wanted the freedom to eat whatever he chose. While he was physically and emotionally stable, Dave presented as relatively able because he was adept at using jokes and distractions to conceal his cognitive limitations. Staff in intellectual disability tend to extrapolate from verbal ability as they strive to match their communication to each person's ability. His apparent verbal ability led to repeated attempts to teach Dave how to calculate his carbohydrate intake and balance this with exercise and insulin. However, formal cognitive assessment by a psychologist found that Dave had no comprehension of number at all so, inevitably, this failed. As his condition deteriorated, he came into conflict with community staff who were trying to guide his food intake. On occasion this had resulted in outbursts including, on one occasion, him running out onto a major road.

A contributing factor to Dave's resistance to staff support was that his father insisted Dave did not have intellectual disability. He told his son and his community support staff that Dave had the right to manage his own money, using threatening language and manner to insist that those staff give Dave his credit card. The acute mental health unit Dave was admitted to when unwell managed this behaviour by sending a lawyer's letter which banned his father from the hospital, on the grounds of unacceptable aggression to staff. It stated that on-site security staff would remove him if he tried to visit.

A repeating pattern was established. A few months after Dave had been discharged well and settled, he would somehow regain access to his credit card and buy food that destabilised his diabetes, necessitating a further admission. Although nobody would confess to this, it was assumed that an inexperienced, isolated or fearful member of staff had acceded to his father's angry demands, since residential staff in the community have neither legal nor security staff to support them. Accepting the complexity of this situation, specialist health services adjusted their goal. Instead of hoping for resolution, they changed this to extending Dave's periods of physical and mental well-being between admissions.

Whenever there is a clash of perspective, service-providers are obliged to find or develop some way to hold the issues and parties in balance. The following summary of another person in the transition research project (Clegg et al., 2017), Tom, describes how what started initially as a difficult move out of school ultimately worked out well for all:

> Tom's mother described him as having a profound intellectual disability with hearing impairment and autistic traits. He had become increasingly difficult to support as he matured physically, being unhealthily overweight and very demanding about food. He slept poorly which meant his parents became exhausted, and assaulted his mother in the mornings as she attempted to wash him.
>
> His parents wanted to continue supporting Tom at home, but their confidence in the appropriateness of this decision was shaken when he became so unhappy during a family holiday that his father had to leave their family group and bring him home. Their confidence was further undermined by choosing a day service for Tom that he did not take to. Then they discovered that a small group home was opening nearby. Its apparently ideal arrangement and location, combined with there being few places that were going quickly, forced them to consider placing Tom out of the family home much sooner than they had originally planned. Moving there transformed his and their life. He stopped overeating, lost two stone, and talked more. He was so much calmer that his grandmother became able to support him at her home for short periods. These changes made his father return to being his previous happy self.
>
> Their transition worker observed that there could have been conflict between home staff and Tom's mother, because at the beginning she phoned or visited many times a day. However, this brought benefits when his TV stopped working. His mother immediately brought him another one, predicting that otherwise he would not sleep and the home would have a difficult night. Staff and mother found a way to respect one another's skills and judgement.

In the literature, accounts of a positive transition from school to adult services such as Tom's are rare, because very few research studies are funded to examine representative samples or total cohorts. In our longitudinal cohort study, while the *process* was as difficult for most parents as previous research had reported, the *outcomes* turned out to be positive for most. While there are plenty of reasons why parents and services may hold a different perspective and struggle to work together, examples of how they do co-operate are rarely documented by a problem-saturated environment.

2   Poverty

This section suggests one way to address the delicate matter discussed earlier. That while services exist to support families that contain a member with intellectual disability, they also have to hold in the back of their mind the possibility that families can be places where neglect, abuse and Adverse Childhood Events damage the person with intellectual disability that services were created to assist (Dion et al., 2018, Vervoort-Schel et al., 2018). One way to escape this dilemma is to identify information that illuminates, in different ways, both horns. Could poverty be a missing link? Recognising that abuse does not only occur in impoverished families, and that most poor families are not abusive, poverty nevertheless affects a high proportion of families involved with intellectual disability mental health services. Living in poverty does make abuse more likely, both within families and from their local communities.

Almost half of families containing a person with intellectual disability referred to mental health services live in disadvantaged areas (48%: Nicholson & Hotchin, 2015), significantly more than would be expected from general population data. Mitigating some of the difficulties those families face would help to avoid the early damage that underpins the distress or dysregulation shown by adults with intellectual disabilities. The following study found that having a child with intellectual disability in the UK is more likely to bring a family into poverty and less likely to allow them to transition out of it, largely because of parents' reduced ability to work. However, this topic has been largely ignored:

> The intellectual disability research community has, with a few notable exceptions, largely disregarded the potential significance of poverty to our understanding of the life experiences of people with intellectual disabilities. (Emerson & Parish, 2010, p. 221)

The impact of poverty was examined in a follow-on study:

Children with intellectual disabilities are ... more likely to be exposed to a wide range of material and psychosocial hazards that are detrimental to their health, including inadequate nutrition; poor housing conditions; exposure to environmental toxins; family, peer, and community violence; poor parenting; and family instability. (Emerson & Spencer, 2015, p. 11)

Social workers used to bring poverty relief into households, and mediate tensions within the family and between it and services, but they are no longer part of multidisciplinary mental health teams in England. Hard-won expertise in providing social care to disadvantaged groups is also being lost under neoliberalism. Specialist social and sports clubs have closed, along with youth worker and social worker posts. In the UK, the few remaining social workers are limited to delivering statutory Mental Health Act roles for the local authority (Stone et al., 2021). In countries such as the UK and Australia, long-term social work relationships have been replaced by a one-touch-and-close, brokerage model of provision where unqualified service planners are expected to deliver whatever users choose, as long as the services benefit the individual with intellectual disability directly. That does not and cannot change complex situations.

Whole-system strategies that enable parents to support their relative with intellectual disability well have been described by family therapists and social workers. Expertise in working with poor families remains relevant (Minuchin et al., 1998; Madson, 1999; Bigby et al., 2018). These advise professionals to adopt an anthropological attitude by using appreciative questions: what is life like for this family, in their locality and situation? What life-goals do they have? Do they recognise resources within themselves or their network that they can call on? Inquiring about the many agencies and professionals in past and current contact with the family can be useful, since there are often too many each doing too little. Instead of adding to the number of people who expect to access a family's private space, streamlining is recommended so that fewer and more effective relationships to develop. A systematic review and meta-analysis found good evidence that early, intensive 'wrap-around' services (Olson et al., 2021) are the best way to reduce poverty and the associated likelihood of abuse that has lifelong consequences.

3   Building a Body of Research That Reflects the Whole Population

Services would become more alert to poverty and its consequences if it was adequately represented in the research corpus, but poor families are harder to reach, often wary of research, and more likely to be buffeted by life-events that make them drop out. Apart from epidemiological research on population data, a remarkably high proportion of intellectual disability research papers contain the following caveat: *The conclusions are limited because the sample comprised relatively well-educated, affluent parents from the dominant ethnic group.* Two issues probably contribute to this.

First, the requirement to demonstrate user involvement. Neoliberal consumerism assumes that the best way to improve services is to ensure they address the concerns of users, which is reflected by research funding bodies. This is particularly problematic when only a narrow range of parents participate. It is further exacerbated by snowballing recruitment strategies, because research-interested graduate parents recruit similar people into the sample from whom data is gathered. In this self-perpetuating system, since the concerns of graduates who choose to get involved differ from parents with fewer educational achievements who live in poverty, the needs and perspectives of disadvantaged families remain unexamined. Despite Emerson's sterling efforts, there appears to be no policy concern about their absence from the published evidence base.

The second reason is the unrealistic expectations of ethics committees. They are properly concerned to protect the interests of vulnerable people with complex needs but do not parse this against their limited capacity to consent. Consequently, preparing and processing research ethics applications is a challenge that can consume much of the first year of a project. In the UK, separate and different types of application are required by university ethics committees, and by formally constituted health and social care ethical committees run by busy senior professionals that meet infrequently. Together, these slow down the pace of research projects significantly. Hollway and Jefferson (2012) observed that ethics requirements for participants to read long protocols and sign multiple consent forms present significant barriers to the recruitment of people from disadvantaged areas. To engage this group, Hollway and Jefferson simply walked around a disadvantaged housing estate knocking on doors. They explained that they would like to interview the resident about what it was like to live in their locality. Since experiencing unfulfilled promises has often damaged trust, the researchers committed to pay them in cash at the minimum wage rate at the end of that interview. Those who agreed to be interviewed had a chance to reflect and change their minds, as the researchers arranged to return later the same day. Such recruitment strategies are likely to be considered too pressurising by ethical committees that vet applications concerning people with intellectual disabilities and mental health problems. That redirects researchers towards inviting volunteers through methods that reach graduate parents most easily: presentations, leaflets and online advertisements. Appointments arranged ahead of time also work best for people with settled lives who use diaries.

While high-risk medical research of course necessitates extremely stringent information-giving and consent procedures, ways to achieve a better balance between the much lower risks associated with social science research and the required information and consent procedures need to be found. In Chap. 4 we drew on an anthropological study by Hubert and Hollins (2006), one of the few to describe the lives and needs of forgotten men with severe intellectual disability living on 'back wards' of a closing institution in the late 1990s. The men could not consent, few had relatives in any contact with the hospital, and almost none had direct contact with their family member. The researchers did have the agreement of hospital staff who knew the individuals, and together they considered it inappropriate to seek consent from family members listed as next of kin who were not in touch. This valuable, low risk project simply involved Hubert reading the men's files, spending a considerable amount of time with them on the ward, and reflecting anthropologically. Nevertheless, at a conference she reported having struggled to publish it: the manuscript had been rejected by some journals because there was no next of kin consent.

In conclusion, the recommendation is that research funders and journal editors fund and publish research that uses representative samples or studies total cohorts, to ensure that those who live in disadvantage and poverty are included. Additional funds to support their discovery and recruitment will be needed. Funding bodies, ethics committees and journal editors also need to achieve a better balance between the level of risk and the stringency of their recruitment and consent expectations. Without these changes, our understanding of the families of people with intellectual disability who live in poverty or disadvantage will continue to be far too limited.

4   Tools to Improve the Relationship

Dunst et al.'s (1994) family-centred approach (FCA) reported a career-long research endeavour about how to work with families effectively, including families of children with intellectual disabilities. This treats the family not the child as the basic unit of analysis; responds to needs identified by the parents not by the professional; and contextualises the family within its network of relationships and resources. The FCA has been positively correlated with parenting self-efficacy, competence and confidence, and positive parental well-being (Mas et al., 2019). It was largely followed for parents of children with intellectual disability in the Netherlands but Vanderkerken et al. (2019) noted two limitations. First and consistent with the intellectual disability research reviewed above, participants were relatively well educated even though this is not typical of the population, and parents' educational level was a significant factor in achieving change. Second, the requirement to focus on strengths clashed with the imperative to address needs, which requires attention to weaknesses.

Research that illuminates parent experiences of services carried out at the University of Leicester, UK is currently under review (Dudley-Hicks, James, & Morgan: contact gsm23@leicester.ac.uk). This started by observing that parents of children diagnosed with an intellectual disability experience higher levels of distress and are sometimes viewed by professionals as problematic or 'lacking resilience'. Since this fails to attend to the distress caused by wider society and the way services are organised, the researchers introduced the British Psychological Society's Power Threat Meaning Framework to a sample of parents. The project explored whether it helped them to create more self-compassionate ways of understanding their experiences of distress or suffering. Moving discussion from 'what is wrong with you?' to 'What has happened to you?', the research identified ways that the *Power* which is pervasive in everybody's' lives caused them difficulty. For example, because they no longer have legal responsibility for their child once they are over 18 information was not shared with parents, they were prevented from making decisions for their child, and professionals used legal power to control services provided. Parents realised that the many *Meanings* they created from what happened to them included feeling silenced, betrayed and overwhelmed. They responded to the *Threats* these presented to their well-being in a wide variety of ways. These included building alliances with professionals; avoiding meetings or walking out of them when feeling overwhelmed; avoiding paperwork; suppressing emotions; normalising or minimising the impact on their lives. Most parents found these discussions enabled them to understand what was happening to them and helped to build resilience.

An assessment process that develops a shared understanding of the socio-emotional needs of children and adults with intellectual disabilities was previously discussed in the review of attachment-based research and intervention (Chap. 4). *The Scale of Emotional Development—Short* (Sappok et al., 2016) is completed by a led discussion between people directly involved with each person. When such discussions include service staff and parents they facilitate a new, shared focus on emotional development rather than behaviour, and create a shared language that enables parents and staff to work together.

New strategies also need to be developed that enable specialist service-providers to steer between two incompatible imperatives: to respect parents as self-determining, and protect people with intellectual disability from harm that originates in the home. Professionals manage this by erecting metaphorical 'Chinese walls' (made of paper so providing no soundproofing but treated as if solid) between different aspects of people in relationship: it is key to successful family therapy with couples involved in domestic violence when the victim does not wish to leave. The following advice drawn from a career providing family therapy to couples caught up in a runaway process of domestic violence may be helpful:

No single paradigm can provide an adequate account of, or an effective treatment for, violence in intimate relationships.... Working with multiple paradigms is not only intellectually necessary, given the complexity of abuse, but is itself a lynchpin of change.... Multiplicity is clinically critical ... *it is the clinician's ability to contain contradictory truths, rather than to choose amongst them that creates the fresh air.* (Goldner, 1999, emphasis added)

When violence in the home is serious enough to call emergency services, those staff should explore whether everybody is safe but their focus is usually limited to the person with intellectual disability and any children present. Yet sometimes it is mothers who are the victims. Maher et al. (2021) found that mothers who faced violence from their adult sons, often those with intellectual disability and autism, got very little support and never from specialists with knowledge of those conditions. Their research concluded that neoliberal states have simultaneously increased maternal responsibility while reducing welfare and social support. Effectively, this has increased mother-blaming.

A new approach to domestic and community violence was developed in Scotland in 2005 after the World Health Organisation dubbed Glasgow the murder capital of Europe. The Scottish Violence Reduction Unit (SVRU) adopted a public-health approach, treating violence as a preventable disease that requires multiple inputs. The government funds local projects based on three underlying, relational principles:

- The active mobilisation of wider community members
- The provision of personal, supportive relationships
- A belief in connection and opportunity as an antidote to violence

Proving cause and effect with social phenomena is always a challenge: these community health projects were supported by tougher sentencing for knife crime and minimum unit pricing to reduce alcohol-related crime. Whatever the relative impact of different strategies, 12 years after the SVRU was created homicides, violent crime, and admissions to hospital for knife wounds had all fallen in Scotland by more than 50%. Since each homicide costs an estimated £1.9 million, and 40% of all public spending goes on such potentially avoidable events, projects can be funded out of savings from crime reduction. A similar argument justifies the costs of 'wrap-around' services for prisoners (Hyatt et al., 2021), and children and adolescents with socio-emotional disorders (Olson et al., 2021). Such approaches are effective and, significantly, more humane not only for the young people and prisoners, but also for the staff and families involved with them. These approaches seem expensive until the social and financial costs of crime and disruption are factored against them.

So, projects need to be initiated with families that contain a member with intellectual disability where violence is an issue, within the home or local community. These would ensure that parents and service staff recognise and respond creatively to relational tensions (Anderson et al., 2020), and examine wrap-around strategies that work well with other vulnerable groups. Knowledge of how to reduce the risk of abuse while maintaining a constructive relationship with disadvantaged families previously developed by social workers should also be re-articulated and retained within practice knowledge.

5   Discover, Encourage, and Create Communities of Solidarity

> Asserting the rights of disabled people and inserting their voice into government bodies is no longer the radical option .... The politically radical option is to attend to similarities between people with intellectual disability, parents and direct care staff .... Since patterns of inequality and domination mark them all, political disruption should aim to dismantle the relevant systems of prejudice. Subtle disruption is more likely to be effective. (Clifford Simplican, 2018)

Attempting to assert the rights of disabled people, and attempting to insert their voice into government bodies has failed to undermine extremes of wealth and poverty created by neoliberalism. That is significant because as the disparity between rich and poor widens, abuse, crime and conflict increase (Wilkinson & Pickett, 2010). Mothers in dangerous situations find themselves 'responsibilised', which mirrors the abandonment of staff that foreshadows abuse previously described in our examination of scandals (Chap. 3). Even in scandals where there is clear management culpability, it is only direct care staff who go to prison.

The radical political action is lower key: refocussing attention onto similarities between people with intellectual disability, parents and direct care staff (Clifford Simplican, 2018). Tava (2023) added a philosophical dimension to this political-epidemiological argument. Solidarity is important because it addresses the welfare of 'consociates' who are linked in an intersubjectively shared form of life. It is impossible to protect the rights and freedoms of an individual without also protecting the community to which that person belongs. Since most consociates of people with intellectual disabilities are over-stretched and experience relative poverty, political disruption should seek to dismantle the systems and beliefs that allow this state of affairs.

Subtle disruption cultivates equal relationships characterised by fun that give a sense of belonging and positive identity for all: people with intellectual disability, staff, and parents. What this could mean was suggested in reflections made by US prison officers who visited a Norwegian maximum-security unit. Part of a project to change punitive, undermanned US prisons into warm, life-changing Scandinavian ones, the visitors were struck by the trust displayed: cells did not have to be locked when people were out of them because items would not be stolen. They also commented on the warmth and absence of hostility:

> One officer emphasized a situation in which the differential approach to staffing became very apparent—recounting an afternoon in which they unexpectedly exercised alongside a group of Norwegian staff and incarcerated men:
> The inmates were doing circuit training and we were invited to come do it with them. … I was welcomed by both staff and the inmates. The inmates were pretty excited to have me in there to see me die. [laughs] I basically died. [laughs] I was sweating all over the place …. But yeah, the training was really fun. The inmates were extremely supportive of one another. But afterwards, none of them came up and made fun of me or anything like that. (Hyatt et al., 2021, p. 1742)

Communities of solidarity are built on the key factor Deleuze found missing from societies that focus on the individual and their achievement of momentary goals: time. It takes enduring relationships to build fun and trust, to develop a working environment that sees little violence. It also takes skill. In Scandinavia, prison staff receive a two-year training, not the five weeks provided for new prison staff in the US.

Communities are characterised by places that Zaha Hadid, an architect influenced by Deleuzean philosophy, called nodes. These are places where people come together, where the possibility of something new can emerge. Community psychologists argue that such places of solidarity exist in the bleakest environments that initially seem to lack co-operative spaces (Kagan et al., 2020). It requires conscious effort to notice and value them, so they send students on their courses out to find such places in their first weeks. They visit community centres, village and church halls, allotments, gyms, libraries with a cafe or nursery attached. Bingo halls, pubs, brass bands and bowling alleys are other possible places of solidarity. There is usually some co-operative present in any locality that can be amplified and supported once noticed and valued: it is much more likely to be enduring than a new initiative introduced by strangers.

Intellectual disability has always had communities of care, but as de-institutionalisation unfolded and gained power they became re-interpreted as negative. Despite this, L'Arche communities have maintained their challenge to standard public services, and there is a rich and growing literature about how and why they are different (McKearney, 2021). Camphill communities also survive, embodying a different approach that makes the built environment fundamental to the psychological environment (McKanan, 2020). While neither L'Arche nor Camphill usually accept people who can be very distressed or disruptive, and professionals can be discomforted by their attention to spirituality, there is still a potential for ideas exchange that could be facilitated.

These approaches have survived despite being widely dismissed as institutional because many parents and people with intellectual disability value the sense of belonging they offer to people who have found little acceptance in geographical communities. One of Camphill's recruiting strategies has been to recruit life-sharing co-workers: providing skilled people with a reason to live in their communities and share their skills. Artists are given studio space and materials to do their own work, in exchange for spending half the week encouraging residents' artwork. In similar vein, people with expertise in music and drama, or sharable skills in gardening and horse-riding have been accommodated and welcomed. This approach has been made more difficult by concerns about abuse and the imposed bureaucratisation of care that is uncongenial to such volunteers. McKanan (2020) records concern expressed about this change. People with skills in arts and performance have been fundamental to therapeutic mental health communities since they first emerged in Italy (Foot, 2015), so it is important not to lose their contribution.

Staying as far under neoliberal scrutiny as possible, some of these communities are exploring new ways to work. A Camphill community for people with intellectual disabilities in Northern Scotland introduced and evaluated social pedagogy, a European approach to development and growth for all. External evaluators from the University of Edinburgh concluded that social pedagogy clearly had a positive impact on both the staff who undertook the training and on the service users (Roesch-Marsh et al., 2015).

In the UK, the College Centre for Quality Improvement's (2013) *Enabling Environments* initiative applies research from therapeutic communities in mental health to develop practice with a wide range of groups. It is a well-developed process of teaching and development that builds supportive exchanges between users and staff but, unusually, also family members—usually parents. This is how it is described:

> An Enabling Environment is one where people work together not only to achieve whatever task that confronts them; but also gain confidence in themselves, enrich their relationships, and experience influencing their environment for the better. It is of course a description of how we would like: our children to be taught, to work ourselves, be treated should we become ill, and even the social club, or religious society, we might belong to.

An enabling environment has ten elements.

1. *Belonging*
   The nature and quality of relationships are of primary importance.

2. *Boundaries*
   There are expectations of behaviour and processes to maintain and review them.
3. *Communication*
   It is recognised that people communicate in different ways.
4. *Development*
   There are opportunities to be spontaneous and try new things.
5. *Involvement*
   Everyone shares responsibility for the environment.
6. *Safety*
   Support is available for everyone.
7. *Structure*
   Engagement and purposeful activity is actively encouraged.
8. *Empowerment*
   Power and authority are open to discussion.
9. *Leadership*
   Leadership takes responsibility for the environment being enabling.
10. *Openness*
    External relationships are sought and valued.

In the UK this has been taken up more by the prison service than mental health or intellectual disability facilities, probably because such innovations have been ignored by the powerful government inspectorate that sets health-related standards. It could bear huge fruit if it were to be promoted and the training and registration process financed. It is currently prevented by institutional faith in PBS as *the* way to support distressed dysregulated people with intellectual disability. As we have emphasised throughout these reviews of evidence and practice, an essential first step would be for intellectual disability to follow child mental health services and make relational continuity one of the major challenges services must meet. That requires attention to the development of constructive relationships not only with distressed people who have intellectual disabilities, but also with and between parents and staff.

6   Conclusion

Dialling down current focus on promoting the autonomy of adults with intellectual disability who are distressed and dysregulated will not come easily. Seeking instead for service staff and parents to co-operate and support one another as well as their sons and daughters is a major culture change. If the boundaries of this new approach were not well-managed, staff could become overwhelmed by the levels of family need they encounter. The final Chap. 6 turns to consider what services might look like in a post-neoliberal world.

References

Anderson, J., Pickard, M., & Rye, E. (2020). The CaPDID training manual: A trauma informed approach to caring for people with a personality disorder and an intellectual disability. Pavilion Publishing. ISBN 978-1-912755-84-4

Baum, S., & Lyngaard, H. (Eds.). (2006). *Intellectual disabilities: A systemic approach*. Karnac.

Bigby, C., Tilbury, C., & Hughes, M. (2018). Social work research in the field of disability in Australia: A scoping review. *Australian Social Work, 71*(1), 18–31. https://doi.org/10.1080/0312407X.2017.1364397

British Psychological Society. Power, Threat, Meaning Framework. (n.d.). https://www.bps.org.uk/member-networks/division-clinical-psychology/power-threat-meaning-framework

Charnock, D. (2014). *You've seen us!': Masculinities in the lives of boys with intellectual disability*. Doctoral thesis, University of Nottingham.

Clegg, J. A., Murphy, E., & Almack, K. (2017). Liberal individualism & Deleuzean pluralism in intellectual disability. *Philosophy, Psychiatry, Psychology, 24*(4), 359–371.

Clifford Simplican, S. (2018). Democratic care and intellectual disability: More than maintenance. *Ethics and Social Welfare, 12*(4), 298–313. https://doi.org/10.1080/17496535.2018.1452954

College Centre for Quality Improvement. (2013). *Enabling environment standards*. https://www.rcpsych.ac.uk/docs/default-source/improving-care/ccqi/

quality-networks/enabling-environments-ee/ee-standards-document-2015. pdf?sfvrsn=abdcca36_2

Dion, J., Paquette, G., Tremblay, K.-N., Collin-Vézina, D., & Chabot, M. (2018). Child maltreatment among children with intellectual disability in the Canadian Incidence Study. *American Journal on Intellectual Developmental and Disability*, *123*(2), 176–188. https://doi.org/10.1352/1944-7558-123.2.176

Dreyfus, S., & Dowse, L. (2020). Experiences of parents who support a family member with intellectual disability and challenging behaviour: "This is what I deal with every single day". *Journal of Intellectual & Developmental Disability*, *45*(1), 12–22. https://doi.org/10.3109/13668250.2018.1510117

Dunst, C., Trivette, C. M., & Deal, A. G. (Eds.). (1994). *Supporting and strengthening families: Methods, strategies and practices*. Brookline Books.

Emerson, E., & Parish, S. (2010). Intellectual disability and poverty. *Journal of Intellectual & Developmental Disability*, *35*(4), 221–223. https://doi.org/1 0.3109/13668250.2010.525869

Emerson, E., & Spencer, N. (2015). Chapter Two—Health inequity and children with intellectual disabilities. In C. Hatton & E. Emerson (Eds.), *International Review of Research in Developmental Disabilities* (Vol. 48, pp. 11–42). https://doi.org/10.1016/bs.irrdd.2015.03.001

Feder Kittay, E. (1999). *Love's Labor*. Routledge.

Foot, J. (2015). *The man who closed the asylums: Franco Basaglia and the revolution in mental health care*. Verso.

Goldner, V. (1999). Morality and multiplicity: Perspectives on the treatment of violence in intimate life. *Journal of Marital and Family Therapy*, *25*(3), 325–336.

Hollway, W., & Jefferson, T. (2012). *Doing qualitative research differently* (2nd ed.).

Hubert, J., & Hollins, S. (2006). Men with severe learning disabilities and challenging behaviour in long-stay hospital care and challenging behaviour in long-stay hospital care. *British Journal of Psychiatry*, *188*, 70–74. https://doi.org/10.1192/bjp.bp.105.010223

Hyatt, J. M., Andersen, S. N., Chanenson, S. L., Horowitz, V., & Uggen, C. (2021). "We can actually do this": Adapting Scandinavian correctional culture in Pennsylvania. *American Criminal Law Review*, *58*(4), 1715–1746.

Kagan, C., Burton, M., Duckett, P., Lawthom, R., & Siddiquee, A. (2020). *Critical community psychology: Critical action and social change*. Routledge.

King, M. (2023). *A socio-legal exploration of the legal and administrative transition to adulthood of people with severe and profound intellectual disabilities in Australia.* Doctoral thesis, Queensland University of Technology.

Madson, W.C. (1999). Collaborative therapy with multi-stressed families. .

Maher, J., Fitz-Gibbon, K., Meyer, S., Roberts, S., & Pfitzner, N. (2021). Mothering through and in violence: Discourses of the 'Good Mother'. *Sociology, 55*(4), 659–676. https://doi.org/10.1177/0038038520967262

Mas, J., Dunst, C., Balcells-Balcells, A., Garcia-Ventura, S., Giné, C., & Cañadas, M. (2019). Family-centered practices and the parental well-being of young children with disabilities and developmental delay. *Research in Developmental Disabilities, 94,* 103495. https://doi.org/10.1016/j.ridd.2019.103495

McKanan, D. (2020). *Camphill and the future: Spirituality and disability in an evolving communal movement.* University of California Press.

McKearney, P. (2021). The ability to judge: Critique and surprise in theology, anthropology, and L'Arche. *Ethnos, 86*(3), 460–476.

Miettinen, S. (2012). Family care of adults with intellectual disabilities: Analysis of Finnish policies and practices. *Journal of Policy and Practice in Intellectual Disabilities, 9*(1), 1–9.

Minuchin, P., Colapinto, J., & Minuchin, S. (1998). *Working with families of the poor.* Guilford.

Namkung, E. H., Greenberg, J. S., Mailick, M. R., & Floyd, F. J. (2018, May 1). Lifelong parenting of adults with developmental disabilities: Growth trends over 20 years in midlife and later life. *American Journal on. Intellectual and Developmental Disabilities, 123*(3), 228–240. https://doi.org/10.135 2/1944-7558-123.3.228

Nicholson, L., & Hotchin, H. (2015). The relationship between area deprivation and contact with community intellectual disability psychiatry. *Journal Intellectual Disability Research, 59*(5), 487–492. https://doi.org/10.1111/jir.12149

Olson, J. R., Benjamin, P. H., Azman, A. A., Kellogg, M. A., Pullmann, M. D., Suter, J. C., & Bruns, E. J. (2021). Systematic review and meta-analysis: Effectiveness of wraparound care coordination for children and adolescents. *Journal of the American Academy of Child and Adolescent Psychiatry, 60*(11), 1353–1366. https://doi.org/10.1016/j.jaac.2021.02.022

Pilnick, A., Clegg, J., Murphy, E., & Almack, K. (2010). Questioning the answer: Questioning style, choice and self-determination in interactions with young people with Intellectual Disabilities. *Sociology of Health & Illness, 32*(3), 415–436.

Pilnick, A., Clegg, J., Murphy, E., & Almack, K. (2011). "Just being selfish for my own sake": Balancing the views of young adults with intellectual disabilities and their careers in Transition planning. *The Sociological Review, 59*(2), 303–323.

Pote, H., Mazon, T., Clegg, J., & King, S. (2011). Vulnerability and protection talk: Systemic therapy process with people with intellectual disability. *Journal of Intellectual & Developmental Disability, 36*(2), 105–117. https://doi.org/1 0.1080/13668250.2011.575771

Roesch-Marsh, A., Cooper, S., & Kirkwood, S. (2015). *Social Pedagogy: Pilot project evaluation.* School of Social Work, University of Edinburgh.

Ryan, S. (2021). *Love, learning disabilities and pockets of brilliance.* Jessica Kingsley.

Saetersdal, B. (1997). Forbidden suffering: The Pollyanna syndrome of the disabled and their families. *Family Process, 36*, 431–435.

Sappok, T., Barrett, B. F., Vandevelde, S., Heinrich, M., Poppe, L., Sterkenburg, P., et al. (2016). Scale of emotional development—Short. *Research in Developmental Disabilities, 59*, 166–175. https://doi.org/10.1016/j. ridd.2016.08.019

Scottish Violence Reduction Unit. (n.d.). https://relationshipsproject.org/ project/48771/

Shakespeare, T. (2014). *Disability rights and wrongs revisited* (2nd ed.). Routledge.

Solomon, A. (2014). *Far from the tree: Parents, children and the search for identity.* Vintage.

Stone, K., McCusker, P., Davidson, G., & Vicary, S. (2021). An exploratory survey of mental health social work in Europe. *International Journal of Environmental Research and Public Health, 18*(19), 10462. https://doi. org/10.3390/ijerph181910462

Tava, F. (2023). Justice, emotions, and solidarity. *Critical Review of International Social and Political Philosophy, 26*(1), 39–55. https://doi.org/10.108 0/13698230.2021.1893251

Todd, S., & Jones, S. (2003). Mum's the word: maternal accounts of dealings with the professional world. *Journal of Applied Research in Intellectual Disabilities, 16*, 229–244. https://doi.org/10.1046/j.1468-3148.2003. 00163.x

Todd, S., & Shearn, J. (1996). Time and the person: The impact of support services on the lives of parents of adults with intellectual disabilities. *Journal of Applied Research in Intellectual Disabilities, 9*, 40–60.

Tomsa, R., Gutu, S., Cojocaru, D., Gutiérrez-Bermejo, B., Flores, N., & Jenaro, C. (2021). Prevalence of sexual abuse in adults with intellectual disability:

Systematic review and meta-analysis. *International Journal of Environmental Research and Public Health, 18*, 1980. https://doi.org/10.3390/ijerph18041980

Vanderkerken, L., Onghena, P., Heyvaert, M., & Maes, B. (2019). Family-centered practices in home-based support for families with children with intellectual disability: Judgments of parents and professionals. *Journal Intellectual Disabilities, 1–17.* https://doi.org/10.1177/1744629519897747

Vervoort-Schel, J., Mercera, G., Wissink, I., Mink, E., van der Helm, P., Lindauer, R., & Moonen, X. (2018). Adverse childhood experiences in children with intellectual disabilities: An exploratory case-file study in Dutch residential care. *International Journal of Environmental Research and Public Health, 15*(10), 2136. https://doi.org/10.3390/ijerph15102136

Voysey-Paun, M. (2017). *A constant burden: The reconstitution of family life (revised).* Routledge.

Wilkinson, R., & Pickett, K. (2010). *The spirit level.* Allen Lane.

Williams, V., & Robinson, C. (2001). More than one wavelength: Identifying, understanding and resolving conflicts of interest between people with intellectual disabilities and their family carers. *Journal of Applied Research in Intellectual Disabilities, 14*(1), 30–46. https://doi.org/10.1046/j.1468-3148.2001.00037.x

6

The Purpose of Exploration is to Arrive Back Where We Started and Know it for the First Time

Abstract This final chapter articulates and coalesces ideas about different futures and possibilities for people with intellectual disability and their carers that have been explored throughout the book. It summarises the need to notice recurring problems that are met with the same response, when a new one is needed if the matter is to be more adequately addressed. It raised consciousness by noticing the pervasiveness of neoliberal individualism, and the sterility of binaries, interventions and tropes that have been deployed for decades. Acknowledging that much thinking and policy in intellectual disability has changed lives for the better, we have argued that 'trying harder' in the entrenched present is not the way forward. Our intention is not to overturn the present assumptive world just to impose a new orthodoxy, but to enter a new period characterised by creativity and experimentation. We bracket matters that are unlikely to change in the short term, to focus on creating and building the alternatives.

Keywords Intellectual disability • Neoliberalism • Bracketing • Creating • Possibilities

1   Noticing

We started by noticing how busy intellectual disability professionals can be, which makes them rush past awkward hedgehogs of doubt that they really need to stop and pick up. Another of psychotherapist Sinason's insights was that professionals who work in intellectual disability make themselves busier than other mental health workers. She wondered if that busy-ness staves off something important. Do we find being unable to cure intellectual disability so unbearable that we work at pace, to reassure ourselves that at least we could not try any harder? So, as well as reflecting on those we seek to help, and about how we offer that help, professionals also need to notice themselves within that whole: their own needs to belong, have fun, do something useful.

Brief narratives about people and situations have been included throughout the book. These are offered to flesh out ideas, teach newcomers something about the field, and inform policy-makers who do not have direct experience of the uniqueness of people with intellectual disabilities. The accounts are not always about problems but they are always about complexity. They are sketched rather than comprehensive, which non-clinicians find alienating but is necessary to protect anonymity. Such accounts do not share the warmth and unique directness of many people with intellectual disabilities, nor the unexpected compassion found in even the most distressed. For that, you could read some of the descriptions in Solomon (2014), who spent a decade interviewing over 300 families about the full spectrum of difference. Some children had intellectual, physical, or sensory disabilities, others were exceptionally intelligent or talented. While he had data on them all he rejected numbers-based conclusions to tell stories, because these acknowledge nuance and chaos.

Our main purpose in including narratives about people and their situation was to help readers grasp how complex the conditions and situations can be for many people with intellectual disabilities and their consociates. These summaries depict the vastly differing situations of the group who are called 'intellectually disabled'. They help to counter simple suggestions that staff should just listen to what people want and provide that, because things are rarely so straightforward. Our vignettes elaborate issues also noticed by other researchers. A study of ageing found that care and support from the state, kin, neighbours, or friends was at best tenuous and at worst disappearing completely, as were places where people could hang out with others (Power & Bartlett, 2019). Once parents had died the wider social networks that they had mediated drifted away from their person with intellectual disabilities; and while siblings and neighbours did offer support, others financially abused or bullied them.

Inevitably, the topic we noticed the most was neoliberal individualism, which is a particularly poor fit for people with intellectual disabilities who need help, support, or care from others. Anthropologists argue that neoliberalism has combined with social media to promote 'cultural homogenisation' (Hornberg, 2023). By analogy with the process that spreads fat globules in milk uniformly, this refers to the way similar ideas have been widely spread and sustained. Guidelines that determine expected health interventions were countered by health professionals like Greenhalgh et al. (2014), who argued that evidence-based medicine fails to consider the efficacy and long-term effectiveness of interventions for people who have multiple conditions. Some of those guidelines are no longer active, because out of date, not least the one that recommended PBS for challenging behaviour in the UK, where the appetite to renew is starting to wane.

An egregious example of the problems that can result from neoliberal inspections that require a particular way of working unfolded when the British Office for Standards in Education (Ofsted) issued a Notice of Complaint to a radical school with an international reputation, Summerhill. This required it to ensure that all children attended lessons (details in Clegg, 2008). However, Summerhill was built on a unique approach developed over decades that education should be non-coercive. Pupils were permitted to miss lessons, but only if they developed an acceptable alternative project and pursued it systematically. Parents likened Ofsted's audit of Summerhill to a game of tennis judged by the rules of basketball. Its former pupils were very positive about their form of education and sufficiently successful to support the school's appeal against this decision, funding a barrister-led appeal at a High Court Tribunal. Evidence about Summerhill's educational performance was provided by an independent evaluation of the school funded by the Nuffield Institute.

After just three days of the hearing, counsel for the Department for Education withdrew its notice of complaint. The final settlement included the barrister's right to be present during the next Ofsted inspection. This rated the education provided by Summerhill *Outstanding*: Summerhill staff responded that they had not changed.

2   Thinking

As a philosophy teacher, Deleuze knew that the ideas people wrestle with initially are the ones that change the way they see the world. Following his perspective on creativity we have sought to bring fresh eyes to topics that demand attention by recurring, while striving to appreciate how all parties are doing their best according to the situation as they see it:

> For Plato, the question is, 'What is x?', for Deleuze, the key questions are 'how many kinds?' 'how?" 'in which cases?' Henry Somers-Hall (2013, p. 193)

'How many kinds?' is an excellent question for intellectual disability, because it is a significantly heterogeneous collective. Its only common factor is that all people whose cognitive impairment is two or more standard deviations below the average are likely to need, and deserve, some level of state support. Yet few policies reflect this broad swathe and mix of different abilities and lives lived. It will require creativity to break out of what seems to be an ossified status quo to embrace multiplicity of ability, circumstance, health need, and kinds of challenge, but creativity is of course difficult. It requires us to see familiar things with new eyes. Travel can help. This book is mostly informed by research and practice in the UK, Northern Europe, and Australia: we invite those more familiar with research from other places to amplify and expand our account. The arts can help too. This chapter title came from poet T. S. Eliot (1968), who famously stated in *Little Gidding* that the purpose of exploration is to arrive back where we started and know it for the first time.

We come full circle by recalling that this book's point of departure was an insight from the originator of neoliberalism, Hayek (1960): that since those who are poor, weak, or vulnerable cannot compete on equal terms, they require additional support that protects them from neoliberal strategies. Hayek was outvoted on this by promoters of his economics, but he was right. Focussing on positive attainments and moments of autonomy is essential and affirming but can lead to a failure to fully understand and honour the subtle, sensitive supports that most people with intellectual disabilities need to develop and sustain a mode of existence that they find acceptable.

We have argued that it is important to notice the many-headed hydra that is neoliberalism, which has tipped the scales too far towards momentary, individual achievements. Moving beyond attempts to insert the voice of individuals with intellectual disabilities into political arenas, the truly radical action is now considered to be created by environments where these persons, along with the staff and families involved with them, subvert the existing order. The new story this mode of existence tells is of belonging, flourishing, and having fun together. We found a word from politics research, their 'consociates', helpful: this may include friends and neighbours but mostly refers to the staff and family members whose engagement is central to these lives. The vision we are building revolves around relationships. These are difficult to develop and sustain in services focussed on individual autonomy that do not value relationships, and employ people on pay scales that do not reward length of tenure.

To articulate this vision, we have sought to cohere and develop strands of intellectual disability research that often originate from less traditional locations. This employs tools for thinking developed by the wider academy particularly history, geography, and anthropology; draws on successful approaches happening in other service systems, such as prisons and education; and is illuminated by insights from families that lend a richness to what is and can be done.

3   Bracketing

Maxwell Jones (1982) created one of the first therapeutic communities in mental health at Dingleton in Scotland. In this memoir, he observed that any leader of a major change has to put energy into what is possible and bracket, that is, put on the shelf anything that seems difficult or currently not open to change. By bracketing the unchangeable that we are compelled to live with, we shrink its size and make it easier to see valuable initiatives and satisfactory lives that are already there, lying in the margins.

Neoliberalism is unlikely to disappear overnight, nor are associated management strategies like inspectorates that monitor against standards that chime with neoliberal values. Bracketing them to run their course sometimes allows newer and emerging approaches to become visible and to flourish. The changes we described as a preferable response to scandals also entails some bracketing. Focussing on the difficult situations many direct care staff have been and still are left in, requires us to bracket our indignation about cruelty. The need to identify and punish outright wrong-doing will still be there, but all the energy should not be expended on that since on its own punishment improves little. The greater priority is ensuring that staff doing difficult and occasionally disheartening work with people who appear unresponsive get the help and support they need to retain their sense of humanity, compassion, and see some progress.

As more people involved with intellectual disability don new lenses, the failure to reflect complexity adequately in single-word service goals and evaluations, and the absence of any room for innovation, should make bracketed issues wither in the face of effective alternatives. Rather than try to replace them with a blueprint, we give air to new ways that services could better meet the needs of people with intellectual disability and their consociates. In the process we seek also to bracket contestation between different types of expertise held by researchers, professionals, the person, and their family, working instead towards communities that are better equipped to hold and respect different kinds of knowledge.

4   Creating

In Chap. 5 we reviewed creative systems of care that energise everybody involved with them. Meeting the ten targets required to register as an Enabling Environment (College Centre for Quality Improvement, 2013) generated places where both prisoners and staff reported feeling safe, engaged, abuzz. It is a shame that there is no example of how an enabling environment would work in intellectual disability, which is not for the want of trying. Clegg and a staff nurse attended seminars on this approach, and attempted to enact this at the acute mental health in intellectual disability unit in Nottingham. However, the year it would have taken to negotiate its introduction with all parties was time that could not be found, because the competing requirement from the inspectorate was to demonstrate that PBS plans were operating there. 'Holidays' from existing expectations need to be possible that allow new approaches to be tried.

Enabling environments are not the only way to engender a creative buzz. Health settings that are research-active often have the same feel, partly because the researchers are up to date with the literature and share both that information and their excitement about the innovation with staff and families. These kinds of projects are springing up in different environments and countries. Here is a recent clinical research project from the Netherlands, to address the needs of people who have intellectual disabilities and whose emotions can be chaotic:

When caring for people with a severe or moderate intellectual disability and behaviour that is difficult to understand, situations can regularly come to a standstill. Although specific methodologies and protocols have been developed, and care professionals often work with incredible perseverance, it does not always happen that one can help the person concerned in a satisfactory manner. Is it time to try something totally different?

To research this question the Centre for Consultation and Expertise together with the VU Medical Centre Dept. of Medical Humanities, the University for Humanistic Studies, Belangenorganisatie KANSPLUS, 7 care organizations, educational programs for Social Work and Nursing and the educational institution for doctors for people with intellectual disabilities formed a 3 year cooperative work relationship.

Healthcare professionals regularly find themselves out of their depth. Since the 1990s, the sector has become increasingly professionalised, and support workers are discouraged from using implicit tools such as emotions, imagination, intuition, and moral knowledge in their daily work. This is remarkable, because these sources of knowledge can be of great value when dealing with challenging behaviour, which is nowadays seen as the result of interactions between the person and their environment. The WAVE project seeks to create more room for this implicit set of instruments. (https://en.projectwave.nl)

Social changes emerging from Europe are challenging neoliberal individualism and competitiveness, by valuing community co-operation and creativity. This recognises that using implicit knowledge based in the emotions, imagination, intuition, and morality, and combining insights from the academy, service systems and consociates, is likely to be a powerful creator of change.

Deleuze (1968) argued that the new often emerges from the margins and the overlooked. Therapeutic communities that showed how mental health services could be different and more humane opened first in the borders of Scotland and on the very edge of Italy, where it meets the Hungarian border (Foot, 2015). A Camphill community outside the northern Scottish city of Aberdeen trialled a European approach to care, social pedagogy (Cameron, 2013), that has been welcomed more widely in child services. This holds that services should go beyond merely instructing or directing residents: everybody should have at least a weekly conversation with someone they trust, who asks them how they are and what they want or need. While it appears to have made no further ground in intellectual disability, it nevertheless offers another possible kind of innovation.

A world-renowned education system developed in Finland, showing how an apparently impossible change can happen by turning teaching into a high-status career (Finnish Education in a nutshell). Only 10% of the people who apply to train as teachers are accepted, and they are trained for much longer than in any other country. A crucial component of this innovation was side-stepping concern about teacher-pupil ratios because that led training colleges to accept people with limited teaching talent. Instead, it was assumed that excellent teachers could manage larger classes. Finland then attracted good teachers by paying them well, and according professional autonomy to both teachers and schools. Assessments are not used to construct league-tables, but to promote self-reflection in pupils who are taught wherever they are best placed. Flexibility is key: children and young people with intellectual disabilities are usually placed in mainstream settings, but there is never one rule for all.

Professional expertise in intellectual disability needs to be given greater acknowledgement, and its staff encouraged to collaborate in integrated and innovative services that work to improve well-being continuously. It was difficult to free staff time to bring evidence-based initiatives like the Enabling Environments project into intellectual disability, because UK inspectors required to see PBS plans. It must become possible for inspectorates to make space for, become curious about, and value other research and innovations.

5   Everything Seems Impossible Until It's Done

This aphorism offers a reminder that change is possible even in times that seem to be entrenched. The current order is held in place by international policies and accompanying monitoring systems that seem unquestionable. People fear being on the wrong side of the debate and either doubt or find out painfully, as Summerhill did, that anything different is unacceptable. But systems of thought do suddenly pivot in a new direction, given multiple prompts and influences. This book seeks to be one such. Can it help to redirect a marshy watershed so that its water fills a different valley? Can it help people to step aside from judgement and the inclination to make scapegoats? Is it possible to look at the next level up and highlight the lack of imagination and lack of resource that limit lives instead?

Our preferred vision arises from considering what happens for people over time and across relationships, bracketing current attention to dominant ideas that have served for decades. It takes a positive view on most of the care provided by both staff and families, while also working to help them build and retain a sense of commitment and humanity whatever their context. It would encourage mutual support, while focussing on actions, interactions, and relationships that endure. We invite all in this field of activity to find and use new ways to see and respond to scandals, distress, and dysregulation; new ways to negotiate and minimise the problems associated with poverty; and to remember that not all abuse stems from poverty. We look forward to learning of new ways of thinking and acting that readers do not find here. Most important is the belief that change is possible, and that hope and fun have their place.

References

Cameron, C. (2013). Cross-national understandings of the purpose of professional-child relationships: Towards a social pedagogical approach. *International Journal of Social Pedagogy, 2*(1), 3–16.

Clegg, J. A. (2008). Holding services to account. *Journal of Intellectual Disability Research, 52*, 581–587. https://doi.org/10.1111/j.1365-2788.2008.01068.x

College Centre for Quality Improvement. (2013). Enabling Environment Standards. https://www.rcpsych.ac.uk/docs/default-source/improving-care/ccqi/quality-networks/enabling-environments-ee/ee-standards-document-2015.pdf?sfvrsn=abdcca36_2

Deleuze, G. (1968). *Difference and repetition* (P. Patton 2004, English Trans.). Continuum.

Eliot, T. S. (1968). *Four Quartets*. Folio Society.

Finnish Education in a nutshell. (n.d.). https://www.oph.fi/en/statistics-and-publications/publications/finnish-education-nutshell

Foot, J. (2015). *The man who closed the asylums*. Verso.

Greenhalgh, T., Howick, J., & Maskrey, N. (2014). Evidence based medicine: A movement in crisis? *British Medical Journal, 348*, g3725. https://doi.org/10.1136/bmj.g3725

Hayek, F. A. (1960). *The constitution of liberty*. Routledge.

Hornberg, A. (2023). The homogenisation of diversity: Processes selecting for biocultural generalism in the Anthropocene. *Swedish Journal of Anthropology, 6*(1), 23–31. http://urn.kb.se/resolve?urn=urn:nbn:se:uu:diva-497384

Jones, M. (1982). *The process of change*. Routledge and Kegan Paul.

Power, A., & Bartlett, R. (2019). Ageing with a learning disability: Care and support in the context of austerity. *Social Science & Medicine, 231*, 55–61. https://doi.org/10.1016/j.socscimed.2018.03.028

Solomon, A. (2014). *Far from the tree: Parents, children and the search for identity*. Vintage.

Somers-Hall, H. (2013). *Deleuze's difference and repetition*. Edinburgh University Press.

Index[1]

---

[1] Note: Page numbers followed by 'n' refer to notes.